COMMODORE PERRY
in the
LAND OF THE SHOGUN

HarperCollins*Publishers*

COMMODORE PERRY
in the
LAND OF THE SHOGUN

by Rhoda Blumberg

Lothrop, Lee & Shepard Books   New York

ALSO BY RHODA BLUMBERG

Shipwrecked!
The True Adventures of a Japanese Boy

Full Steam Ahead:
The Race to Build a Transcontinental Railroad

The Incredible Journey of Lewis and Clark

What's the Deal?:
Jefferson, Napoleon, and the Louisiana Purchase

Commodore Perry in the Land of the Shogun
Copyright © 1985 by Rhoda Blumberg
All rights reserved. No part of this book may be used or reproduced in
any manner whatsoever without written permission except in the case
of brief quotations embodied in critical articles and reviews. Manufactured in
China. For information address HarperCollins Children's Books, a division of
HarperCollins Publishers,
1350 Avenue of the Americas, New York, NY 10019.

Library of Congress Cataloging-in-Publication Data
Blumberg, Rhoda.
 Commodore Perry in the land of the Shogun.
 Bibliography: p.   Includes index.
 Summary: Details Commodore Matthew Perry's role in opening Japan's
closed society to world trade in the 1850s, one of history's most significant
diplomatic achievements.
 ISBN 0-688-03723-2 — ISBN 0-06-008625-4 (pbk.)
 1. United States Naval Expedition to Japan (1852–1854)—Juvenile
literature.   2. United States—Foreign relations—Japan—Juvenile literature.
3. Japan—Foreign relations—United States—Juvenile literature.   4. Perry,
Matthew Calbraith, 1794–1858—Juvenile literature.   [1. United States Naval
Expedition to Japan (1852–1854).   2. United States—Foreign relations—
Japan.   3. Japan—Foreign relations—United States.   4. Perry, Matthew
Calbraith, 1794–1858.]   I. Title.
DS881.8.B53   1985   84-21800
952'.025

Visit us on the World Wide Web!
www.harperchildrens.com

For my husband, Gerald
and my son, Lawrence

I want to thank my friend Dorothy Segall, who helped me
acquire some of the illustrations and supplied me with source
material from her private library.
I'm also grateful for the guidance of another dear friend
Amy Poster, Associate Curator of Oriental Art
at the Brooklyn Museum.

• TABLE OF CONTENTS

Steamships were new to the Japanese.

PART I

THE COMING OF THE BARBARIANS

The Black Ships arrive,
July 8, 1853.

1 • ALIENS ARRIVE

IF MONSTERS HAD DESCENDED UPON JAPAN the effect could not have been more terrifying.

People in the fishing village of Shimoda were the first to spot four huge hulks, two streaming smoke, on the ocean's surface approaching the shore. "Giant dragons puffing smoke," cried some. "Alien ships of fire," cried others. According to a folktale, smoke above water was made by the breath of clams. Only a child would believe that. Perhaps enemies knew how to push erupting volcanoes toward the Japanese homeland. Surely something horrible was happening on this day, Friday, July 8, 1853.

Fishermen pulled in their nets, grabbed their oars, and rowed to shore frantically. They had been close up and knew that these floating mysteries were foreign ships. Black ships that belched black clouds! They had never seen anything like it. They didn't even know that steamboats existed, and they were appalled by the number and size of the guns.

Barbarians from out of the blue! Will they invade, kidnap, kill, then destroy everything? What will become of the sacred Land of the Rising Sun?

General alarms were sounded. Temple bells rang, and messengers raced throughout Japan to warn everyone that enemy aliens were approaching by ship.

Rumors spread that "one hundred thousand devils with white faces" were about to overrun the country. People panicked. They carried their valuables and furniture in all directions in order to hide them from invading barbarians. Women and children were locked up in their homes or sent to friends and relatives who lived inland, far from the endangered shore.

Messengers rushed to the capital of Edo (now Tokyo) to alert government officials. Edo, the world's largest city with more than one million occupants, went into a state of chaos the very day the ships were sighted. Women raced about in the streets with children in their arms. Men carried their mothers on their backs, not knowing which way to turn.

Who could control the turmoil? The Emperor Komei was isolated in his royal palace at Kyoto. Although he was worshiped as a divine descendent of the sun goddess, Amaterasu, he was a powerless puppet, responsible primarily for conducting religious ceremonies. During his leisure hours he was expected to study the classics and compose poetry. The Japanese referred to their emperor as "he who lives above the clouds." By law, he was not permitted to leave his heavenly palace unless he received special permission from the government. An emperor's sphere of influence was otherworldly. All down-to-earth decisions were made by shoguns who had been wielding power for more than 700 years.

The word *shogun* means "barbarian expelling generalissimo." How appropriate at this time! Surely the Shogun would take command!

But Shogun Ieyoshi who occupied the palace at Edo in 1853 was a weakling. No one even bothered to tell him the frightening news. Three days after the ships arrived he overheard chatter about them while enjoying a Noh play that was being performed for him in his palace. The news affected him so badly that he went to bed, sick at heart.

Because the Shogun was inept, his councillors, called the *Bakufu,* ruled the country. But according to a Japanese reporter, "They were too alarmed to open their mouths."[1] The Bakufu should not have been so surprised. Before reaching Japan the American fleet had stopped at Loo Choo (now Okinawa). Japanese spies stationed there had sent word that American ships were on their way to Japan. Dutch traders had also alerted the Bakufu. But for mystifying reasons, the government did not take these reports seriously until the Black Ships arrived on July 8. After recovering from shock they ordered the great clans to prepare to battle barbarians.

Locked away from the rest of the world, using the Pacific Ocean as its moat, Japan had maintained a feudal society similar to that of Europe during the Middle Ages. There were lords *(daimyos)*, knights *(samurai)*, and vassals who labored in their lord's domain and paid tithes to their masters.

The country had not been at war since it invaded Korea in 1597. That was 256 years earlier. Nevertheless, feudal lords were able to mobilize troops. Men who had never dressed for warfare worked to get rust off spears. They placed new feathers in their families' antique arrows. Tailors were pressed into service so they could fix the silk cords on ancient armor, make warriors' cloaks, and sew cotton skull-

A samurai readies for battle.

caps that would cushion the weight of heavy helmets. Seventeen thousand soldiers were readied for battle.

When the ships moved toward land that first day, Japanese guard boats set out to surround the enemy. But they could not catch up with aliens whose ships were so magical that they steamed ahead against the wind without using sails or oars.

At five o'clock in the afternoon the foreign ships anchored a mile and a half from shore, at Edo Bay. They were less than thirty-five miles from the capital city. Beautiful cliffs, rolling green hills, and, above all, snow-capped Mount Fuji made a breathtaking scene. After dusk, beacon fires dotted the land, and there was an incessant toll of temple gongs.

That night a meteor with a fiery tail streaked through the sky like a rocket. An omen from the gods! Shrines and temples were jammed. Priests told worshipers that barbarians were about to punish them for their sins.

The *Susquehanna* was a steam-powered sailing ship.

2 • THE BLACK SHIPS OF THE EVIL MEN

FOUR SHIPS AND 560 MEN of the U.S. Navy had created this furor. The *Mississippi* and the *Susquehanna* were steam-powered. The *Plymouth* and the *Saratoga* were three-masted

sailing ships in tow behind the steamers. The Japanese referred to these four vessels as "The Black Ships of the Evil Men."

Commodore Matthew Calbraith Perry was in command of the squadron. He had not come to invade. He hoped to be a peacemaker who would make the isolated Empire of Japan a member of "the family of civilized nations"[1] of the world. His mission was to unlock Japan's door. It had been slammed shut against all but a few Dutch and Chinese traders, the only ones officially allowed in for over 200 years.

Perry expected to deliver a letter from President Millard Fillmore to the Emperor of Japan, proposing "that the United States and Japan should live in friendship and have commercial intercourse with each other."[2] The letter requested that ports be opened so that American ships could obtain coal and provisions. (See Appendix A.)

America had invested seventeen million dollars in the Pacific whaling industry, and it needed Japanese ports to replenish coal and provisions for the whalers. Whale oil was essential for lighting and for lubricating machinery.

President Fillmore's letter also asked that men who had been shipwrecked on Japanese shores be treated with kindness. This point was emphasized because many American whaling ships had been wrecked off Japan's coast by violent storms, and their castaways had been jailed and abused.[3]

Perry intended to deliver the letter and sail away peacefully. He would winter in Hong Kong. With only four ships and supplies that could last no more than one month, he would not attempt to wait for the Emperor's reply, but he planned to return in the spring—when he would have more supplies and a larger fleet.

The Commodore was determined not to use force unless attacked. But he felt that he could not trust the actions of unknown Orientals. He dared not take chances, for he remembered the *Morrison,* an American ship that had sailed

THE COMING OF THE BARBARIANS

Commodore Matthew C. Perry

into Edo Bay on a peaceful mission in 1837. Its intent was to return seven Japanese castaways to their homeland. The Japanese had opened fire and forced the ship to leave.

As a precaution, Perry's squadron anchored in battle formation facing the shore. Cannons and guns were loaded. All hands took up their battle stations.

Japanese guard boats approached the moored American ships. Each vessel, propelled by six to eight standing oarsmen, was filled with about thirty soldiers. Fastening ropes to the ships, they tried to climb on board. Commodore Perry ordered his sailors to cut the guard boats' ropes and use pikes and cutlasses to keep the Japanese away. A few tried to climb the *Mississippi*'s anchor chain. A rap on the knuckles sent one soldier into the water. All of the Japanese soldiers howled and shouted angrily.

Perry's stubborn refusal to allow them on board was based on the terrible experience of another American commodore. Seven years before, in 1846, Commodore James Biddle had anchored at Edo Bay, hoping to deliver a letter to the Emperor from the United States government. The letter requested trade relations between the two countries. As a friendly gesture, Biddle allowed swarms of Japanese soldiers to come aboard. A rude soldier gave Biddle a shove that knocked him off his feet. Anxious to keep peace, Biddle graciously accepted an apology, which was interpreted as weakness and cowardice. Japanese officials mocked him, refused to deliver documents, and ordered him to leave at once. Because his orders were not to create an incident, Biddle immediately sailed away.

Perry resolved that until negotiations were successful, he would not allow more than three officials on board at a time.

A Japanese guard boat rowed close to the Commodore's flagship, the *Susquehanna*. Its men held up a scroll, written in large letters, in French, that said, "Go away! Do not dare to anchor!" Then one of the Japanese shouted in English, "I

Interpreter Antón Portman, drawn by an
unknown Japanese artist

can speak Dutch."[4] He asked to come aboard. Antón Portman, Perry's Dutch-Japanese interpreter, came on deck. He
explained that the Commodore would only allow the highest officials on his ship. When told that there was an important person in the guard boat, he lowered a gangway ladder.

Nakajima, introduced as vice-governor of the small
nearby village of Uraga, climbed up. In fact, Nakajima was
not a vice-governor but merely a minor official. He was
accompanied by a Dutch-speaking interpreter.

Commodore Perry secluded himself in his cabin. He
refused to be seen by a vice-governor or, indeed, by any but
the most important emissaries of the Emperor. Lieutenant
John Contee was told to speak with Nakajima. Contee explained that the Commodore's intentions were friendly.
Perry merely wished to present a letter from the President

of the United States to the Emperor of Japan. Nakajima replied that the American ships must go to the port of Nagasaki, where there was a Dutch trading post so that the Dutch could act as go-betweens.

Through his lieutenant, Perry let it be known that he would never go to Nagasaki and if all guard boats didn't disperse immediately there would be trouble. Nakajima went to the gangway, shouted an order, waved his fan, and all guard boats except his own departed at once. When Nakajima took his leave he promised that a higher official would see Perry the next day, Saturday, July 9.

That night, when the meteor streaked across the sky, Perry noted in his journal that this was a favorable omen: ". . . we pray God that our present attempt to bring a singular and isolated people into the family of civilized nations may succeed without resort to bloodshed."[5]

3 • HIS HIGH AND MIGHTY MYSTERIOUSNESS

AT DAWN THE AMERICANS were amazed to see a boatload of artists near the *Susquehanna.* Using fine brushes, ink stones, and rolls of rice paper, they were making sketches of the ships and any of the crew they could see. Their curiosity was obviously stronger than their fear. Within a week, pictures of the Black Ships and "hairy barbarians" were hawked in the streets and sold in shops. They were also reproduced on souvenir banners, scrolls, fans, and towels.

While these artist-reporters were acting like war correspondents, the coastline was bustling with activity. Women and children carrying baskets of dirt helped men build new

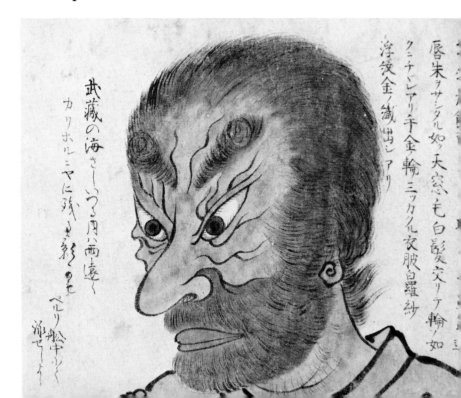

Another Japanese view of
Commodore Perry

The Japanese artist entitled this picture *Portrait of a High Official of the North American Republic.*

fortifications. Thousands of soldiers marched to and fro while their leaders decided upon strategic battle positions. They displayed colorful banners emblazoned with their lords' arms. Some trained muskets on Perry's squadron. Strips of canvas had been set up along the coast to hide these activities, but the Americans could see over them. The sailors were amused and dubbed the canvases "dungaree forts."

At seven o'clock in the morning, Kayama, so-called "governor" of Uraga, was welcomed aboard the *Susquehanna.* Actually he was *not* a governor but a police chief. Uraga's real governor, who did not wish to meet barbarians, gave Kayama permission to take his place. Dressed for the occasion in an embroidered silk robe, a lacquered hat with padded chin straps, and clunky clogs, this little man looked comical and ill at ease, even when his Dutch interpreter introduced him as a person of great importance.

Commodore Perry would not see him. He secluded himself in his cabin again, for he rightly guessed that Kayama was not an eminent envoy of the Emperor. Because he remained hidden like a holy man, the Japanese soon spoke of Perry as "The American Mikado," and called his quarters "The Abode of His High and Mighty Mysteriousness."[1]

Commanders Franklin Buchanan and Henry Adams spoke with Kayama. The conversation was awkward because it had to be translated from English into Dutch and then into Japanese, and back again. Perry's son Oliver acted as go-between. On board as his father's secretary, he rushed to and fro with orders for Buchanan and Adams, and reports for his father.[2]

Kayama insisted that the Americans had to go to Nagasaki. He explained that Japanese law made it impossible for a letter to be received at any other port. Perry refused to budge and threatened to deliver the letter in person at the royal palace in Edo. Frightened at the thought, Kayama

The Commodore's son Oliver Perry *(left)*; Commander Henry Adams *(right)*.

promised to contact the Emperor, then timidly asked why four ships were needed in order to carry one little letter to the Emperor. "Out of respect for him," Perry retorted.[3] (The Commodore had no way of knowing that the Shogun occupied the Edo palace, and that the Emperor was a powerless figurehead who lived in Kyoto surrounded by the Shogun's spies.)

Kayama became even more alarmed when he noticed that small boats launched from the ships were cruising close to the mainland. He exclaimed that the Americans were violating Japanese law. The officers countered by saying that they were obeying American law. They had to survey coastal waters—a preparation in case Perry decided to land.

During the surveys one of the Americans looked at some Japanese soldiers through a telescope. The soldiers ducked, probably believing that the spyglass was a new type of gun.

Strange music came from the ships on Sunday, July 10. The crew sang hymns, accompanied by a band whose instruments were unheard of in Japan. A boatload of Japanese asked to visit, but they were refused admission because Sunday was the Christian day of rest.

On Monday morning surveying boats were sent farther than ever up Edo Bay. Kayama came aboard in a panic. The activities of the Americans had caused great distress in Edo, because the city's principal food supply depended upon boat traffic. Fear of the foreigners prevented supply boats from sailing.

Despite Kayama's pleas, the Americans continued to chart the coastal waters. Their survey boats came near enough to fortifications to observe that they were made of dirt and wood. There were a few cannons, but they were small and old. Most of them were 8-pounders, 200 or 300 years old, and they had not been used for a long time. The Japanese probably did not even know how to fire them. One of Perry's crew quipped that he could load all the Japanese

Surveying parties met Japanese guard boats on Monday, July 11, 1853. (At left, a Japanese coastal junk.)

cannons into the American 64-pound cannons and shoot them back.

Soldiers loyal to two daimyos requested permission to shoot at the Americans. Fortunately, their lords decided to hold fire, thus preventing an incident that might have started a war.

Although officials were terribly alarmed, many ordinary citizens calmed down after the first day of shock. A few hailed the men in the surveying boats and offered them water and peaches. A Japanese guard boat welcomed some of the surveyors aboard. The Americans amused and fascinated their hosts by shooting Colt revolvers in the air.

The Americans were enchanted by the kindness and friendliness of the Japanese. At one time they believed that

HIS HIGH AND MIGHTY MYSTERIOUSNESS

27

they had sailed over the edge of world civilization and would encounter savages. Face to face, they were beginning to realize that these charming people were as courteous and hospitable as any they had ever met. They were yet to discover that Japan was a highly civilized, cultured nation.

Early in the morning on Tuesday, July 12, Kayama went to the Americans and again asked them to go to Nagasaki. Through his intermediaries Perry stated that if the President's letter was not answered soon he would "consider his country insulted and will not hold himself accountable for the consequences. He expects a reply of some sort in a few days, and he will receive such reply nowhere but in this neighborhood."[4]

Kayama rushed back to Uraga to consult with officials, then returned that afternoon. He announced that a building would be erected on shore for a reception and a very important person would receive the letter.

Kayama and his companions then relaxed, especially after accepting drinks of whiskey and brandy. They became red-faced and merry, yet their manners remained elegant, their curiosity insatiable. Perry permitted them to tour the ship and examine its guns and engines.

Unlike the general population, Kayama's interpreters knew something about Western science and world geography. Their knowledge of the Dutch and Chinese languages enabled them to learn facts about forbidden lands across the sea. They asked about roads that cut through mountains and about a railroad that was being built across the isthmus of Panama. When a globe was placed before them they immediately pointed to Washington and New York.

It was seven o'clock in the evening before the Japanese left the ship, bowing every step of the way. The Americans were impressed with their politeness, and noticed that when the Japanese were in their own boats en route to shore, they were as formal, elegant, and dignified with each other as they had been with the Americans. Proper etiquette was not "company manners" but typical behavior.

On Wednesday, July 13, Kayama came aboard to exhibit a document from the Emperor. It authorized important officials to meet with Perry. The royal message, wrapped in velvet and encased in a sandalwood box, was treated with such reverence that Kayama would not allow anyone to touch it. Instead, the Americans were given a translation. The document specified that His Highness Toda, "Prince of Izu," and Ido, "Prince of Iwami," were authorized to receive the President's letter. These "princes" were actually the governors of Uraga.

Oriental duplicity? Not just Oriental! The Americans knew the art of bluffing, too. During the talks with Kayama they called Perry "admiral," because the title was more impressive than that of commodore, which is a lower rank.[5]

4 • LANDING ON SACRED SOIL

INSTEAD OF USING ONE of their permanent buildings, the Japanese erected a temporary wooden structure for their meeting with the Americans. It was located in a small village near Uraga.

At daybreak on Thursday, July 14, the *Susquehanna* and the *Mississippi* moved close to land, anchored, and aimed their guns at the shore. The men were prepared for battle in case their landing party was attacked.

Kayama came aboard as official host. He was dressed for the occasion in a costume made of multicolored silk, yellow velvet, and gold lace. Kayama may have looked magnificent by Japanese standards, but the Americans had to suppress their laughter. His trousers were so short and wide that the sailors thought they looked more like a petticoat.

All members of the crew were eager to set foot on Japanese soil, but since the ships had to be manned, they drew lots to determine who would go ashore. Fifteen launches carried about 100 marines, 100 sailors, and 40 musicians. Japanese guard boats flanked the Americans. As was customary, their oarsmen hissed as they rowed.

The American sailors and marines wore blue and white uniforms, officers were in full dress, and all were heavily armed with cutlasses and guns. As for "Admiral" Perry, his heavy uniform was buttoned to the throat despite the hot July weather. Tall and elegant, with sword at his side, he did indeed look like a Lord-High-Everything.

Perry proved to be a first-class showman, for he planned and staged a dramatic entrance. First, the marines formed two lines on the wharf. Then came sailors, marching to the lively music of two bands. Ships' cannons saluted when Commodore Perry disembarked. Bands played "Hail, Columbia" when he landed. Perry was flanked by two tall handsome black bodyguards, who proved to be sensational. The Japanese had never seen black men before.

The Americans could not have been more startled if they had traveled in a time machine to King Arthur's kingdom. The shore was a scene of feudal splendor. Thousands of Japanese soldiers encased in armor lined the beach. Some were pikemen. Others were archers, equipped with eight-foot bows. Two-sworded samurai warriors were everywhere. Lines of cavalry were stationed behind foot soldiers. Heraldic banners held high represented the daimyos to whom their soldiers owed allegiance. According to their tradition, warriors' faces had to look fierce. A few soldiers wore ferocious-looking masks that had been designed to scare enemies. The soldiers glared and glowered as the Americans marched by.

In the background villagers milled about, jumping up and craning their necks to get glimpses of the barbarians. The officers' uniforms with gleaming buttons and the wide epaulettes amused them. They never dreamed that clothing of this sort existed. Nor had they ever seen men with such long noses or with brown, blond, or red hair. And their size! The aliens were giants compared to Japanese men, who averaged five feet one inch. (Just as medieval European knights were shorter than modern men, nineteenth-century Japanese soldiers were smaller than today's average Japanese male.)

OVERLEAF: *The First Landing of Americans in Japan,* July 14, 1853

THE COMING OF THE BARBARIANS

LANDING ON SACRED SOIL

The Audience Hall

The Commodore and his officers entered a canvas tent that served as an anteroom, then walked a carpeted path to the main hall. The walls were draped with huge purple silk banners displaying the imperial coat of arms. The floor was covered with red cloth.

The Americans did not know that ten samurai were underneath, concealed beneath the floor, ready for a signal to rush out and kill Perry and his aides.

As soon as Perry entered, the "princes" Ido and Toda rose from low stools and bowed. The Americans were seated on chairs that had been hastily taken from a nearby temple. Buddhist priests sat on these when they conducted funeral services. Only then did they dangle their legs from chairs, because the Japanese usually kneeled and sat back on their heels—a posture that Westerners still find difficult.

President Fillmore's letter was encased in a beautiful rosewood box with locks and hinges made of gold. When the Commodore signaled, two ship's boys carried the box to his bodyguards, who, in turn, placed the letter in a scarlet container supplied by the Japanese. A letter from Perry with Dutch and Chinese translations was also presented.

Kayama approached Prince Ido, got down on all fours, bowed his head to the floor, then received a Japanese document. He took it to the Commodore, then prostrated himself once again before "His High and Mighty Mysteriousness."

Perry had not expected any written reply. His Dutch interpreter, Portman, explained that the document was merely an imperial receipt. It stated: "The letter of the President of the United States of North America and a copy are hereby received and will be delivered to the Emperor. . . . Therefore, as the letter has been received you can depart."[1]

The entire procedure lasted about twenty minutes. Ido

The delivery of President Millard Fillmore's letter

and Toda never uttered a word, because speaking with foreigners was against the law. A long silence was broken when Perry announced through his interpreters that he expected to leave in two or three days, and that he would return in the spring. "With all four vessels?" the Japanese interpreters asked.

"All of them," Perry replied, "and probably more, as these are only a portion of the squadron."[2]

The fleet departed on July 17, three days after the meeting on shore, nine days after the arrival at Edo Bay.

Before the Americans sailed away, Kayama came on board

bearing presents of food, fans, pipes, and soup bowls. In turn, Perry gave him calico, sugar, wine, and books. At first Kayama was reluctant to receive gifts. Owning foreign objects was forbidden. However, he couldn't resist. He concealed the books and bottles in his capacious gown. After bowing farewell to his American friends, he left with tears in his eyes. Kayama's mood became less sad after he entered his own boat. He knocked off the neck of a wine bottle and drank its contents.

Poor Kayama was punished. Ido destroyed his gifts and had him demoted because he had been too friendly with the Americans.

Perry was proud of his accomplishment. Nearly sixty years old, he had added to a long and distinguished career. As an officer in the U.S. Navy he had hunted pirates and slave traders. He had successfully commanded the largest American naval force during the Mexican War (1846–1848). He had succeeded in peace talks with Mexican leaders and African chiefs. He modernized the navy by insisting upon steam-powered warships. But he knew that his Japanese encounter was more significant than any of his former achievements. Both Russia and England had attempted to open Japanese ports for foreign ships and failed. Although Perry was unwelcome and overwhelmed in numbers, he had dared to land on the sacred soil of a hermit nation. He was the first Western ambassador to be received in Japan in over 200 years. How proud he was that he did not have to fire one shot!

In a letter to his wife Perry wrote, "This achievement of mine I consider an important event in my life. The Pageant was magnificent, and I am the only Christian that has ever before landed peacefully on this part of Japan or any part without submitting to the most humiliating degradation."[3]

The Commodore was referring to the Dutch, who were then being humiliated by the Japanese.

5 • THE DUTCH ISLAND PRISON

ALTHOUGH THE DUTCH were permitted to run a "factory" (trading station) near Nagasaki, they lived like prisoners. They were confined to Deshima, a tiny fan-shaped island in Nagasaki harbor. It measured 200 yards long and 80 yards wide. The mainland was only a few yards away, but a high wall blocked their view of it. A stone bridge outside the wall connected Deshima with Nagasaki. This was guarded by soldiers who allowed only those with special permits to pass.

No more than twelve or thirteen Hollanders lived on Deshima at a time. Wives and children were not allowed to stay or even visit with them.

The Dutch were allowed to hire Japanese servants and workers. But in order to be employed on Deshima, these people had to use their own blood to sign an oath pledging not to become friendly with the Dutch. They were not to reveal any information about their country, no matter how trivial. They were not to converse with Hollanders, but were to speak only when words were necessary to do their jobs. By law they returned to Nagasaki before sunset. The bridge gate was locked from dusk to dawn.

The only other occupants on the island were police-spies, and a few Japanese interpreters. Japanese scholars visited the tiny island occasionally in order to learn news of the outside

Picture of a Dutchman

world. On Deshima they could obtain books about the arts, customs, and scientific advances in Europe. They were particularly interested in medicine and astronomy.

The Dutch could not leave their island prison without special permission, which had to be obtained at least twenty-four hours in advance. If someone wished to take a walk in the streets of Nagasaki, he had to be accompanied by numerous interpreters and officials, who, in turn, invited friends to join the group. A stroll on the mainland often entailed being escorted by thirty Japanese. If two Dutchmen obtained permission to visit Nagasaki, the number accompanying them doubled. And they were expected to buy everyone an expensive dinner! It was hardly worth it. Only boredom brought them to take an excursion to Nagasaki.

Once a year, in the spring, the factory director and a few of his staff journeyed to Edo to pay homage to the Shogun. The trip took three months: one month going, one month at Edo, and a month returning. Spies assigned to accompany the Dutch saw to it that they did not detour or mingle with natives. Even while traveling they were quarantined.

More than a hundred servants were needed to transport their clothing and furniture. Chairs, tables, china, silverware, and European wines and foods were brought along so they could enjoy one of their few pleasures: dining in Dutch style wherever they lodged. The pilgrimage was a financial drain, because in addition to their travel expenses, they were obliged to bring expensive gifts to the Shogun.

When they arrived in Edo, the Dutchmen were confined to their rooms and guarded by spies. They waited, sometimes for weeks, until notified that the Shogun wished to see them at his castle.

After sending gifts of cloth, liquor, maps, and books, plus a written report about world affairs, they humbled themselves before the Great Lord of the Land. As soon as they entered the palace's Hall of One Hundred Mats, they crawled across the floor on their hands and knees, bowed at the Shogun's feet, then retreated by backing out on all fours. No one dared to look around the room, fearing that such curiosity would seem disrespectful.

The entire procedure took a few minutes. It was demeaning, but not as humiliating as performances some Dutchmen were forced to put on in the past. To amuse the Shogun, they had been ordered to jump, dance, sing, act drunk, clown, and kiss each other. If they wanted to continue trading, they had to do whatever stunts the Shogun wished. Exporting copper, iron, gold, silks, and lacquerware and importing European goods such as firearms, fabrics, tobacco, and spectacles were sufficiently profitable for them to submit to the Shogun's degrading games. Playing the fool was worthwhile, even though the Dutch were restricted to the arrival and departure of one ship a year.

Commodore Perry knew about the Dutch at Deshima through a book called *Manners and Customs of the Japanese*. It was written by a German physician, Philip von Siebold, who was employed by the Dutch at Deshima in the 1820s. Von Siebold had accompanied the Dutch to the Shogun's court. He was eventually expelled by the Japanese, possibly because he learned too much about the Forbidden Land.[1]

6 • FOREIGNERS FORBIDDEN

THE JAPANESE hadn't always been cut off from the rest of the world. Before they shut their doors in the seventeenth century they traded with foreign countries. China, Korea, Cambodia, Siam, and even the distant Philippine Islands were visited by Japanese trading ships. Japan also welcomed ships from Europe.

The Portuguese were the first Europeans to land in Japan —*Cipango,* the fabulous country that Columbus had hoped to reach. They arrived in 1542, when one of their ships was driven off course by strong winds. The Japanese welcomed the Portuguese, especially because they supplied guns.

In 1549 Christianity was introduced by the Portuguese Jesuit missionary St. Francis Xavier. Spanish friars soon followed and set up missions. As a result, thousands of Japanese were converted.

In 1600 the first Englishman reached Japan. He was Will Adams, the pilot of a Dutch ship that landed in Japan with only twenty-four survivors out of a crew over a hundred. Because of Adams's knowledge about the outside world, Shogun Ieyasu declared that he was too valuable to be allowed to return to England. He became the Shogun's interpreter, tutor, chief shipbuilder, and adviser. The Shogun made him a samurai and arranged for him to have a Japanese wife. (You may be familiar with Adams's story. He was the hero, Blackthorne, in James Clavell's novel, *Shogun,* which was dramatized on television.)

Adams made a point of telling the Shogun about the conquests of England's enemies, Spain and Portugal. He spoke about Spain's invasion of America and the Philippines, and Portugal's seizure of the East Indies. Shogun Ieyasu had always suspected that Spanish and Portuguese missionaries were advance agents plotting aggression, and his new English adviser was eager to confirm his suspicions. In 1614 Ieyasu expelled all foreign priests and missionaries.

After Shogun Ieyasu died in 1616, Christianity was banned on penalty of death. Ghastly persecutions of Christians followed. Stamping on the cross became an annual ceremony. Even during the nineteenth century, Dutch merchants, castaways, and Japanese families who had once been converted were forced to trample upon holy Christian symbols. Those who refused were killed.

The English and Dutch were permitted to trade. They were tolerated because they were not "selling" religion. In 1623 the English stopped doing business with Japan because it was not profitable. Only the Dutch were left. By 1641 the Japanese had confined them to Deshima, the small trading post in Nagasaki harbor described in Chapter 5.

To insure isolation, a series of laws decreed:

- No Japanese could go abroad.
- No shipwrecked Japanese could return home from abroad.
- No foreigners would be tolerated.
- No large ships could be built. Only small boats could be constructed, conforming to a specified design that made them incapable of long voyages.

Sealed against foreign contacts, the general public knew nothing about the existence of the United States. They had never heard about the French Revolution or the Industrial Revolution. They hadn't even seen pictures of steam engines, railroads, telegraphs, and modern firearms. Only select scholars and statesmen knew about events and advances that took place in Europe and America.[1]

Americans and Europeans didn't know very much about Japan. Many thought that it was an obscure Pacific island inhabited by backward, barbarous people.

Gathering information about Japan had been an important part of Commodore Perry's preparations. Before leaving the United States he traveled to upper New York State, Massachusetts, Pennsylvania, and Washington, D.C., collecting books and interviewing people. He asked whaling captains about the offshore waters of Japan, and he interviewed seamen who had been shipwrecked and imprisoned by the Japanese. The Dutch helped Perry. They supplied maps of Japan by handing them to the American minister to the Netherlands. But Perry never learned about Japan's political organization.

Like all officials of the United States government he thought that "emperor" and "shogun" meant the same person. And although he became familiar with some aspects of their society, he did not understand their culture and unique social structure.

7 • THE GREAT PEACE

PERRY ARRIVED during the Tokugawa Period. Shoguns belonging to the Tokugawa family that ruled Japan after 1603 had deliberately preserved a medieval feudal society. Laws, customs, even fashions hadn't appreciably changed for 250 years. Although there were occasional rice riots due to food shortages, there were no major revolts. Because the country had isolated itself against foreign contacts, no wars took place. The Tokugawa Period was also known as "The Great Peace."

The rewards of peace were many. Domestic trade prospered. Castle towns developed into cities. There were five large universities for lords and samurai, and many local schools were set up by lords for their vassals. The literacy rate in Japan during the mid-nineteenth century was probably higher than that of most European countries. Almost half the male population could read and write.

The arts flourished. It was a time of great novels, philosophies, plays, poetry, paintings, and woodblock prints. The Great Peace was a golden age of culture and creativity.

How mistaken Commodore Perry was in his belief that Japan was uncivilized. Although technologically behind the West, no other country in the world was more civilized and artistic. Nor was any government anywhere more highly organized.

The Great Gate at Edo, in the theatrical district

However, the price paid for this productive peace was complete loss of freedom. Life was wretched for most of the population. People were obligated to obey rigid rules that covered every aspect of their existence. The goods they could buy, the size and type of houses they could legally dwell in, the persons to whom they must bow, were all specified by law. Regulations listed 216 varieties of dress for everyone from the emperor down to the lowest class citizen. Even the shape, color, and size of stitches were specified. Those who disobeyed risked severe punishment.

Each person's status was fixed by inheritance. There were four classes ranked below the daimyos. In order of importance they were the warriors *(samurai)*, the farmers, the artisans, and the merchants. The merchants were low on the list because they were viewed as unproductive—mere middlemen who prospered from the labors of others. The only people beneath the merchants were called the untouchables *(eta)*, who were not considered a class. They were the undertakers, tanners, and butchers. These people were also "uncountables" and were not included in the census. The land they occupied was not officially measured. Untouchables were treated like ghosts who did not really exist.

Codes of laws regulated the activities of all, from the Imperial Court down to the merchants and untouchables.

The Emperor

Laws of the Imperial Court specified that the emperor must devote his time to studying the classics and upholding the traditions of poetry. In addition to his role as religious leader, he was expected to confer ranks and titles (upon those who met with the shogun's approval). Although none denied his lofty position and he was revered as a god, he was, nevertheless, treated like a prisoner of the shogun. The divine ruler was usually confined to his palace grounds, where he was spied upon. A law forbade any but an official of the shogun from conveying messages outside the Imperial Palace. The punishment for anyone else who attempted to see the emperor was exile.

The Shogun

As "barbarian expelling generalissimo" the shogun was expected to protect the nation against foreigners. In theory, his greatest duty was to carry out the wishes of the Imperial

Court. In practice, he was the power behind the throne. Rules of conduct and codes of laws had been formulated by shoguns. As a result, a shogun was not subject to strict regulations.

The Lords

Laws for the Military Houses applied to daimyos. These lords could not marry without the shogun's approval. The number of their vassals and the size of their castles were regulated by law. They were forbidden to socialize with

A daimyo

people outside their own domain. (This prevented plots against the government.) They were required to pay for repairing castles, roads, and fortifications not only on their own territory but in other parts of the country. (This kept them from becoming too wealthy and powerful.) The Rule of Alternative Attendance was the most repressive of all. It required that all lords spend part of every other year at Edo, near the shogun. When they went home to their own castles, they had to leave their wives and children in Edo as hostages. (This assured obedience to the shogun.)

There were about 250 daimyos in Japan when the Americans arrived. Approximately 350,000 samurai served as their noble knights.

Samurai

The samurai were masters of the farmers, artisans, and merchants. They organized these underlings into groups of five families. Each person in the group was responsible for the good behavior of others. All risked punishment if one person in a unit did not pay taxes, work diligently, or show proper respect to a superior.

A samurai wore two swords. A smaller one was wielded when cutting off the head of a defeated rival. It was also used for *seppuku,* ritual suicide. (The slang word is *hara-kiri,* which means "belly splitting.") A samurai was always prepared to die by disemboweling himself should his or his lord's honor be tainted. Seppuku was considered to be particularly well done if the samurai composed a poem before or while committing suicide. A close friend often helped end the agony by beheading the samurai after he had disemboweled himself.

The longer sword, the sharpest in the world, could cut through iron nails or split an enemy in two from head to

Japanese artist Shunyei's print
of a samurai in peacetime

Two samurai, sketches in ink and wash by Yoshitoshi

foot. It was occasionally useful in times of peace, for a samurai enjoyed "the right of killing and going away." A law decreed: "Common people who behave unbecomingly to a samurai or who do not show respect to their superiors may be cut down on the spot."[1] Inferiors who did not bow quickly enough could lose their heads.

Despite his power, a samurai was completely dependent upon his daimyo, who gave him a meager salary. Forbidden to work or to become involved in any commercial enter-

THE COMING OF THE BARBARIANS

prise, he therefore had no trouble obeying the rule that to be virtuous he must live a frugal, simple life. During The Great Peace, samurai managed their lords' estates and supervised the repair of public highways and buildings.

A samurai was not expected to be merely a fierce warrior. According to his code, "The arts of peace on the left hand and the arts of war on the right. Both must be mastered."[2] A samurai was encouraged to be scholarly and enjoy the arts. Despite his fierce demeanor, he delighted in parties devoted to moon watching, cherry blossom viewing, poetry, flower arranging, and incense scenting. Many were outstanding scholars, poets, and painters.

By the nineteenth century nearly every domain had a school for samurai. Each student was categorized according to his family's importance, and strict regulations defined his rank. At one school, for example, the student from an important family was expected to be accompanied by one servant who held his umbrella in case of rain, and another who guarded his sandals while he attended lectures. Lower-class samurai children carried their own umbrellas and checked their sandals with a school servant. Some fiefdoms had more than thirty classifications of samurai, each required to follow specific rules of conduct.

Ronin were samurai warriors without lords. Many were cultured, law-abiding citizens. Others were ruffians who roamed the countryside as highway robbers.

Farmers

Farmers made up 80 percent of Japan's nineteenth-century population of thirty million. Each farmer's rank was determined by the amount of rice he grew. A harvest of 500 bushels, for example, entitled him to have a large home—provided it had no parlor and the roof was not tile. A

100-bushel harvest meant a tiny hut with no floor mats.

A farmer was forbidden to drink saki or smoke tobacco. The types of lanterns, flowerpots, clothes, and even the quality of the dolls his children played with were all decreed. He had to wear cotton clothes, not silk—even if he raised silkworms. A law specified the exact day he had to change from summer to winter garments and vice versa, regardless of the weather. He could not travel outside his district without special permission. He was often recruited to do highway work, without pay, which meant that he was forced to neglect his own fields. And he had to give anywhere from 40 to 80 percent of his crops to his daimyo! As a result, most farmers were poverty stricken.

A Japanese farmer

THE COMING OF THE BARBARIANS

Artisans and Merchants

Towns and big cities like Kyoto, Edo, and Osaka were centers for the lower classes, the artisans and merchants. The artisans were superb craftsmen. They made lacquerware, forged swords, wove fabrics, and produced porcelains and papers that were unmatched in quality and beauty anywhere in the world. Shopkeepers sold these unique items to the wealthier daimyos and to courtiers of the Imperial Palace.

Huge stores that sold goods to the general public used business techniques similar to those used today. Their merchandise was advertised, prepackaged, and price-tagged. Many shopkeepers became rich. Businessmen who bought, sold, and shipped foodstuffs and goods also accumulated fortunes.

Nevertheless, merchants, like the rest of the population, had to act with caution. Sometimes those who flaunted their wealth by living luxuriously were denounced and had their businesses confiscated. The government became the new owner. Spies pretending to be customers were always ready to report merchants who criticized official policies.

Although ancient laws supposedly controlled their lives, the merchant class started to become emancipated from rules because their superiors needed their help. Not only samurai but daimyos and officials of the shogun borrowed money from them. Many upgraded their status by paying money in order to become samurai. They were also "adopted" as sons by samurai who owed them money or who wished to have a rich member in their family.

By the mid-nineteenth century the stratified class system was breaking down. Merchants were becoming powerful and influential because they financed many daimyos. Many businessmen were anxious for foreign trade and opposed to the government's isolation policy. Scholars and political activists also wanted to end the country's seclusion. Therefore, Perry's proposals were seriously considered.

8 • CLOUDS OVER THE LAND OF THE RISING SUN

SHORTLY AFTER COMMODORE PERRY'S SHIPS sailed away, the Shogun's advisers distributed translations of President Fillmore's letter to all the daimyos and asked for their opinions. This was unprecedented. Never before had a Tokugawa government asked feudal lords for advice. But the shogunate realized that while the country was in no position to defend itself against a foreign power, it could not maintain a seclusion policy without risking war. The Shogun's councillors hoped that the daimyos would recommend a treaty with the Americans, and therefore take the responsibility for ending isolation.

The daimyos consulted scholarly samurai before writing recommendations. A few welcomed trade with the United States, while some wanted to postpone the decisions so the country could strengthen its defenses. Others insisted upon maintaining the country's complete isolation, even if it meant war.

"Revere the Emperor; Repel the Barbarian" was a slogan that rallied support for activists who opposed the Shogun. These radical isolationists wanted to overthrow him and restore the Emperor to power. They believed that the Shogun had "lost face" when he allowed foreigners to land on

THE COMING OF THE BARBARIANS

sacred soil. He no longer deserved a title that meant "barbarian expelling generalissimo."

Aizawa Seishisai, one of the leaders of the anti-Shogun faction, wrote, "Our Divine Land is situated at the top of the earth. The Americans occupy the hindmost region of the earth. Thus its people are stupid and simple." According to his geography, all Western countries occupied "the lowly organs of the legs and feet of the world."[1] He warned that these feet trampled on other countries. If the barbarians were permitted to trade, they would try to victimize Japan the

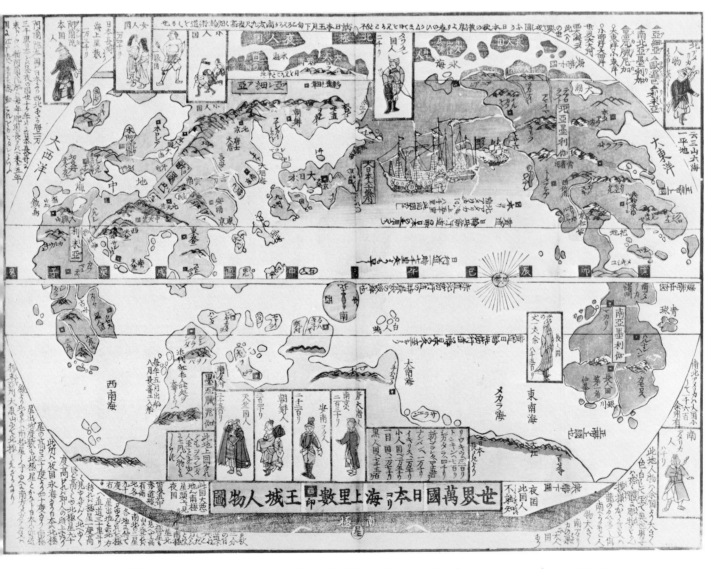

This old Japanese map of the world reads "From Japan, North America is about 500 ri [Japanese miles] distant with no countries between. Holland is 13,000 ri distant. Countries of women only, pygmies, and one-eyed people are respectively 14,000, 15,000 and 17,000 ri distant." A North American is pictured in the upper right hand corner.

way Britain had victimized China during the Opium War (1839–1842) when their warships had bombed and captured Chinese cities, forced China to open ports, and made Hong Kong a British Crown Colony.

One of the daimyos, the Prince of Mito, melted temple bells in order to cast new cannons. He sent a number of these to Edo to be used against the Americans, stating, "If we don't drive them away now, we shall never have another opportunity."[2]

"Eastern Ethics, Western Science" was the motto of scholars who favored an American treaty. They admired the West because of its accomplishments in science, industry, and armaments. They reasoned that the government's financial problems might be remedied by overseas trade. And they realized that their country's poorly trained army and old-fashioned cannons were no match for Perry's precision-drilled soldiers and his modern weapons. The group advocated opening Japan's doors to America and other foreign countries.

Yoshida Shoin, a samurai who was one of their leaders, was convinced that Japan must learn Western technology as quickly as possible, yet still hold on to the moral values of Japanese civilization. He studied "Dutch learning" at Nagasaki, and yearned for a chance to travel and obtain first-hand information from the West, which he would use to enlighten his countrymen.[3]

The Emperor was given a copy of President Fillmore's letter. This was most unusual, for the divine ruler of the Land of the Rising Sun was not supposed to be bothered with current events. But the government was so distressed at the crisis caused by the Black Ships that it hoped the Emperor would ask the gods for help.

When Emperor Komei saw a copy of the letter, he exclaimed that the barbarians should never again be allowed on Japan's sacred soil. After ordering priests to conduct special

A samurai
dressed in armor

THE COMING OF THE BARBARIANS

Emperor Komei

worship services at the Shrine of Ise dedicated to the sun goddess, he offered his own prayers, requesting a *kamikaze* ("divine wind") hurricane that would smash the American ships. (A heavy gale did make the going rough for Perry's fleet, one day after it left Japan.)

The Shogun's advisers were in a quandary. They realized that they could not wage a successful war against the Americans. Yet they feared that signing a treaty could mean the collapse of their government. However, as a precaution, they repealed the law against building large ships and ordered several warships from the Dutch. They also turned for advice to a Japanese who had lived in America for ten years.

The Japanese-American

Manjiro had been a poor fisherboy of fourteen when he was shipwrecked on a deserted island. An American whaler rescued him, and the ship's captain adopted him, brought him to Fairhaven, Massachusetts, and enrolled him in school under the name of John Mung. (Manjiro sounded too foreign and was hard to pronounce.) He subsequently became first mate on a whaler and took part in the California gold rush, where he managed to dig up a modest amount of pay dirt.

Manjiro loved America, but he became homesick and yearned to see his mother again. He arranged for a ship to drop him off at Nagasaki. He risked his life, aware that Japan's Exclusion Edict decreed that "He shall be executed who went to a foreign country and later returned home."

When he arrived at Nagasaki, Manjiro was imprisoned and had to stamp on the cross as proof that he had no intention of practicing Christianity. He stood trial eighteen times! However, because of his vast knowledge of America, he was considered too valuable to kill. Not only was he released, he was made a samurai.

After Perry arrived, the Shogun sent for Manjiro, the only man in the realm with first-hand knowledge of the United States. Although some members of the government wanted him to be the official interpreter at the Treaty House, others opposed this. They insisted Manjiro must not be permitted to meet the Americans. They felt he was too sympathetic to the United States because he had been treated so well by the barbarians "he owes a debt of gratitude to them."[4]

He told the Shogun's councillors that "it has been a long cherished desire on the part of America to establish friendly relations" and that "they [the Americans] have no desire to take land from another country."[5] He described the aliens as "sturdy, vigorous, capable and warmhearted people." But he cautioned the Shogun that "there are hardly any foreign weapons that can frighten Americans out of their wits."[6]

Manjiro's descriptions of life in America entertained, intrigued, and changed the attitude of his superiors toward the "foreign devils." He took some of the mystery away from the exotic lands of North America by reporting strange customs. The following remarks of Manjiro are recorded in official documents:

> When a young man wants to marry he looks for a young woman for himself without asking a go-between to find one for him.
>
> For their wedding ceremony, the Americans merely make a proclamation to the gods, and become married, after which they usually go on a sightseeing trip to the mountains. They are lewd by nature, but otherwise well-behaved.
>
> American men and women make love openly. [They kiss in public.]
>
> A man takes off his hat when paying a visit. He never bows . . . he sits on a chair instead of the floor.
>
> It is customary to read books in the toilet.
>
> American women have quaint customs. For instance, some of them make a hole through the lobes of their ears and run a gold or silver ring through this hole as an ornament.
>
> The women do not use rouge, powder, and the like.
>
> A mother . . . gives of all things, cow's milk as a substitute for mother's milk. But it is true that no ill effects of this strange habit have been reported.[7]

Many historians are positive that Manjiro's influence helped bring about America's treaty with Japan. Were it not for him, Perry's mission might have failed. Even though he was not allowed to leave Edo, Manjiro played a vital role during all subsequent negotiations.[8]

A Superb View of the United States Squadron, Under the Command of Commodore Perry, Bound for the East shows the fleet that returned to Japan on February 13, 1854.

PART II

THE RETURN OF THE BARBARIANS

9 • THE BLACK SHIPS RETURN

COMMODORE PERRY HAD TOLD THE JAPANESE that he expected to return in the spring, with a larger fleet. While waiting for more ships, his squadron docked at Hong Kong, known as the "man o'war's paradise"—plenty of women and liquor. In order to maintain control, Perry saw to it that officers drilled their men regularly, and he insisted that his crew arrange decent entertainment on board the ships. Musicians from the *Mississippi* gave concerts. The *Susquehanna* featured its Troupe of Funny Fellows, whose comical shows had female characters "appropriately wigged and dressed." (Costumes were expertly and inexpensively made by Hong Kong's cheap labor.) Men aboard the newly arrived *Powhatan* featured the Ethiopian Minstrels. (Minstrel shows were the rage in pre-Civil War America, in both the slave states and in the North. Entertainers blackened their faces in order to caricature poor, uneducated blacks. There were skits, jokes, and song-and-dance routines.)

The *Powhatan*

The Shogun had died ten days after the Americans left Japan.[1] At the request of the Japanese government, the Dutch informed Perry that there would be a long period of national mourning, and, therefore, he should not return in the spring. The Commodore suspected that the death was an excuse for delaying his return.

Russians who had heard of the Shogun's death sent word that the Japanese would not receive foreigners for at least three years. Perry feared that the Russians wanted to detain him while they hastened to Edo for their own treaty. After learning that a French ship docked near Hong Kong had suddenly put to sea under sealed orders, Perry decided to move on. Neither the Russians nor the French would get ahead of him. Rather than wait for spring and good weather, he left as soon as he organized his expanded fleet, braving the rough seas and extreme cold that made winter sailing dangerous.

On February 13, 1854, the Americans reentered Edo Bay and anchored near Uraga. They had nine heavily armed ships, with approximately 1,600 men.

Japanese officials and interpreters came aboard the *Powhatan,* which Perry had made his flagship for this visit. Weeks of long, tiresome talks took place about where the Americans should land. Perry, sequestered in his cabin, once again played the role of His High and Mighty Mysteriousness. Commander Adams, designated to represent him, stated that

Commodore Perry and Commander Adams

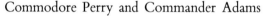

THE RETURN OF THE BARBARIANS

"Admiral" Perry wished to negotiate a treaty at Edo. However, he was told that a Treaty House had already been erected at Uraga.

Talks dragged on day after day until the Commodore lost patience and let it be known that he intended to march to the Imperial Palace. According to a Japanese interpreter, he threatened to make war, and "in the event of war he would have fifty ships in nearby waters and fifty more in California, and that if he sent word he could summon a command of one hundred warships within twenty days."[2]

In order to relieve tensions, Commander Adams invited the Japanese to bring their wives on board ship for a dance. The reaction was unexpected, and the invitation certainly changed their serious mood, for the Japanese could scarcely suppress laughter. What a ridiculous idea! Bring *wives* to a dance? Americans have absurd, amusing customs.

But many Japanese were not so amused when they heard a 21-gun salute on February 22. This was part of the crew's Washington's Birthday celebration. Frightened villagers didn't calm down until they were told that the shots were in honor of the "King of America."

On the other hand, Americans were alarmed and grasped their sidearms when a Japanese official snapped his fan shut. It sounded like a pistol shot. They relaxed only after the fan carrier put on spectacles in order to read documents.

During the long three-week wait at least eight boats left the American ships every day to survey and chart the waters. The crew took turns. Despite the harsh winter weather, the men were happy to leave the monotony of shipboard life. To break up the boredom, Perry saw to it that band concerts were frequent. (He had hired an Italian bandmaster who was in charge of the quality and performance of the music.) The crew was encouraged to fish, not so much for food, but in the hope of discovering new species. The Commodore was very interested in natural science. Whenever an unusual fish

American
musicians
on shore leave

Fishing was a popular pastime.

was caught, an artist on board painted its picture before it ended up on a galley's stove.

Twelve days after the Black Ships appeared off Uraga, Kayama showed up. The officers were delighted to see him. He had played such an important role during their first visit, they wondered why he hadn't been sent out to greet them. Some feared that he had been ordered to commit suicide because he had been too friendly with them. However, although his government was piqued by his attitude toward the Americans, they summoned him at this time because he got along so well with them. Perhaps he would be able to convince Perry to land at Uraga.

Because the talks weren't making headway, Perry ordered his ships to sail toward Edo. Kayama received instructions from his alarmed superiors: "If the Americans land at Edo, it will be a national disgrace. Stop them and have the meetings at Kanagawa."[3] Kanagawa was near Yokohama, which was a small fishing village at that time. (Today Kanagawa is part of the city of Yokohama.)

The deadlock ended. The Treaty House was transported from Uraga piece by piece and set up in the new location, closer to Edo. Perry anchored his squadron in Yokohama Bay in battle formation, heavy guns covering five miles of shore. Commanders Buchanan and Adams were sent to Kanagawa to examine the site of the Treaty House and to instruct native workmen about building a wharf suitable for the navy's boats.

Parties

On March 1, the Americans gave a party for Japanese officials. Kayama and nine other guests enjoyed the experience of eating strange foods using odd-looking utensils—knives, forks, and spoons. They drank cherry cordial and champagne, served in the most unusual containers they had ever seen—glassware. One fellow filled his glass with olive oil and drank heartily, assuming it to be a type of wine. (What a belly laugh the Americans had! But the tables were turned when weeks later a navy man tasted Japanese hair oil, then bought some believing it was good liquor.)

A Navy man tasting Japanese hair oil

The guests wrapped leftover turkey, asparagus, ginger, pie, and other desserts in pieces of paper that they always carried in their wide sleeves. Bringing home leftovers from a banquet was an accepted custom. But the crew thought them crude and made fun of "Japs in silk petticoats" who wrapped food in "nose papers." (Their all-purpose tissues were useful as handkerchiefs and made excellent writing and wrapping paper—finer than any made outside the Orient.)

Several more parties were given for the Japanese while all waited for the Treaty House to be completed. To prove that they were a hospitable people, one of the Japanese mentioned that after a treaty was signed, the crew would enjoy the company of Japanese women. But he advised them to shave off their moustaches, because the females did not like hairy men.[4]

At one of these get-togethers, Kayama was introduced to

Thought to
represent
Sam Patch

a Japanese member of the crew, called Sam Patch. (No one knew his Japanese name.) Patch had been shipwrecked, then rescued by an American merchant ship. After spending a year in California, he went to China and there joined the crew of the *Susquehanna*. He did so without intention of returning to live in his native land.

When Patch met Kayama he was terrified. Trembling with fear, he fell to his knees, positive that he was about to be condemned and beheaded for allying himself with aliens. Commander Adams had a hard time convincing him to stand up, assuring him that as a member of an American crew he was safe from harm.[5]

10 • THE TREATY HOUSE

THE TREATY HOUSE was completed on March 8, 1854. From his ship Perry could see that the building was surrounded by cloth screens. This upset him, and he remarked that the enclosure reminded him of a prison yard. He immediately sent an officer ashore to demand that the screens be removed. They were hastily folded up and taken away, much to the amusement of the crew, who laughed at the "cloth fortifications." In reality, these screens displayed the coat of arms of the local daimyo and were intended as decorations.

Five Japanese commissioners were at the Treaty House ready to start the talks. Crowds had kowtowed on their hands and knees, noses touching the dirt in order to honor the arrival of these officials.

A group of colorfully costumed samurai and their underlings were stationed at the entrance of the Treaty House. Lieutenant George Preble described them in a letter to his wife: "The retainers of the great chief in their heraldic dresses bring one back to the feudal ages. I saw the retainers of one chief yesterday wearing cloaks with broad red and white stripes with a blue patch on the shoulder so that they looked not unlike a walking regiment of American flags. The retainers of another chief wore cloaks with blue and white checks, six inches square—walking chessboards."[1]

OVERLEAF:
Americans landing
at Yokohama,
March 8, 1854.

Some 500 American seamen and marines and 3 ships' bands proceeded to shore in 27 boats. Perry took no chances. All men, even the musicians, were armed with swords and pistols.

When they landed, they formed two lines, marines on the left and seamen on the right. Officers waited on the wharf to greet the Commodore and upon his arrival they escorted him to the Treaty House as bands played "The Star Spangled Banner." The music, the splendor of the officers' full-dress uniforms, and the precision of their parade made an imposing show. As a climax, Perry arranged a 21-gun salute in honor of the Emperor, then a 17-gun salute in honor of the

Entering the Treaty House.

Japanese dignitaries. As a further compliment, a three-striped Tokugawa flag was hoisted to the masthead of the U.S.S. *Powhatan.*

The Treaty House was made of unpainted white pine and had paper windows. It was adorned with colorful tassels and streamers. Despite these decorations, Lieutenant Preble wrote that the building looked like a coal shed. There were magnificent temples that could have been used for the meeting. But the Japanese were not about to taint their sacred structures with foreign devils. And besides, the Commodore had insisted upon a location on flat land within cannonshot of his ships. A farmer's wheat field had been chosen for the site.

Japanese officials escorted Commodore Perry, his son, Oliver, Commander Adams, and interpreters Samuel Williams and Antón Portman into the building. The American and Japanese delegates were seated on benches facing each other. Tiny cups of tea, candies, and small pipes of tobacco were passed around.

A rough sketch by William Speiden, Jr., purser of the *Mississippi,* shows the meeting in the private audience room with the Americans seated left and the Japanese seated right.

Chief interpreter Yenosuke started the talks. He kept bowing, crouching, and crawling back and forth between the commissioners and the Commodore in order to converse with them. Interpreter Williams found Yenosuke's groveling "repulsive," and wondered, ". . . what respect can a man have for himself in such a position?"[2] He could not realize that Yenosuke was conducting himself according to the proper etiquette of his people. Greatly respected as a scholar, Yenosuke had been summoned from Nagasaki, where he had learned to speak fluent Dutch. He also learned a smattering of English from shipwrecked American sailors who had been held in Nagasaki.

Communicating was time-consuming and difficult. Perry spoke to interpreter Portman who spoke Dutch to Yenosuke who crept across the room to translate the conversation into Japanese. Then the reverse procedure took place.

Interpreter Samuel Williams

Interpreter Williams's services were not needed at this time, for he was Perry's expert in the Chinese language. Williams wandered outside the Treaty House where he was kept busy autographing samurai's fans, using Chinese characters. Williams did not use Western letters because the Japanese could not make head or tail of our side-winding script. (Our handwriting looked like messy scribbles. Their calligraphy, on the other hand, reminded sailors of the clawprints of chickens that had walked across paper.)

A long scroll was handed to Perry. This proved to be a reply to President Fillmore's letter that had been delivered the previous July. The scroll, which addressed the Commodore as "Ambassador," was to "His Majesty the President." It stated that answering all the Americans' requests was "positively forbidden by the laws of our Imperial Ancestors." But it agreed to supply American ships with coal, wood,

The Commodore

water, and other provisions. The document even mentioned that Japan was willing to open up one harbor—but not for about five years. It also stated that shipwrecked seamen would be treated well. (See Appendix B.)

Hayashi, a professor from Edo University who acted as chief commissioner, commented that his government would not open the country for foreign trade. At this time, Perry was not concerned about establishing trade relations. He was more interested in emphasizing the plight of shipwrecked sailors. He warned that if castaways continued to be treated cruelly there could be war. Hayashi declared that Perry's information about Japan's behavior toward foreign prisoners was false. He told the Commodore that Americans could be inhumane. They slaughtered thousands of people on the battlefield. The Japanese, by contrast, had not waged war for almost three centuries. Therefore, Japan placed a higher value on human life than America did.

This gave Perry pause for thought. It is possible that at this time he recalled reading about the ritual suicides that seemed to make life cheap. Along with samurai and soldiers, patriots protesting government policy, officials who made mistakes, people who could not pay their debts, students who failed, and lovers who could not marry gained honor through ritualized self-destruction.

Although suicide was repugnant to him, Perry had paid tribute to a self-sacrifice that would have been laughable from a Japanese point of view. In 1853, when Perry was on his way to Japan, he made a stop at Mauritius, an island in the Pacific near Madagascar. He and his officers visited a monument in honor of a lady and her husband-to-be who went down with a ship that sank in 1744. The woman could have saved herself by removing some of her voluminous clothing in order to swim to the nearby shore. But she refused out of modesty. Her fiancé chose to stay by her side, and they drowned together. Modesty, honor, self-destruction! On Mauritius, these values seemed romantic to Perry.

But during his talks with Commissioner Hayashi, the Commodore was in no mood to engage in a conversation about the value of human life. Negotiating a treaty was uppermost in his mind. He told Hayashi that if this could not be accomplished, the United States would probably send more ships, but he hoped that everything would be settled in a friendly manner.

Perry remarked that a treaty similar to the one made between the United States and China would be satisfactory. This treaty opened ports and guaranteed special privileges for Americans. The Chinese treaty and two notes from Commodore Perry were left for the commissioners to study.

11 • AN ARRAY OF GIFTS

IN ORDER TO WIN OVER THE JAPANESE, the Commodore depended not only on the power of his fleet but also on the goodwill he would generate by presenting his hosts with an overwhelming assortment of gifts. Perry had spent months choosing and ordering them before he left the United States.

While documents were being translated and studied the time seemed appropriate for gift giving. Captain Joel Abbot of the S.S. *Macedonian* was in charge of delivering the presents with proper ceremony. The gifts filled several large boats, which were sent to shore with other boats occupied by officers, marines, and a band playing music. A building next to the Treaty House had been erected especially to display the many presents.

Gifts for the Japanese

The commissioners received lists of the items and the names of the persons who were to receive them. The Emperor, the Empress, and the five commissioners were the principal recipients. There were lifeboats, books, maps of America, whiskey, wines, clocks, cloth, rifles, swords, pistols, pictures, perfumes, mailbags, potatoes, seeds, and a large array of agricultural equipment. (See Appendix C.)

Captain Joel Abbott

The farm tools attracted crowds. Important Japanese were invited to handle them. When a grindstone was set up, some samurai took out their short swords to test how well they could be sharpened. One of the Americans demonstrated a folding ladder and showed how a long-handled pruning saw worked. A garden engine-and-hose proved so intriguing that some Japanese amused themselves by dowsing treetops with water. Then they drenched a crowd of spectators, who dispersed, laughing. Everyone thought it was great fun.

The hose and folding ladder were especially important for their firefighters. In a land where walls were made of wood, windows of paper, and roofs of thatch, housefires were commonplace. The poetic name "Flowers of Edo" referred to fires that "blossomed" nightly, lighting up parts of the big city.

A half mile of telegraph wire was strung from the Treaty House to a nearby building. One of Perry's lieutenants had

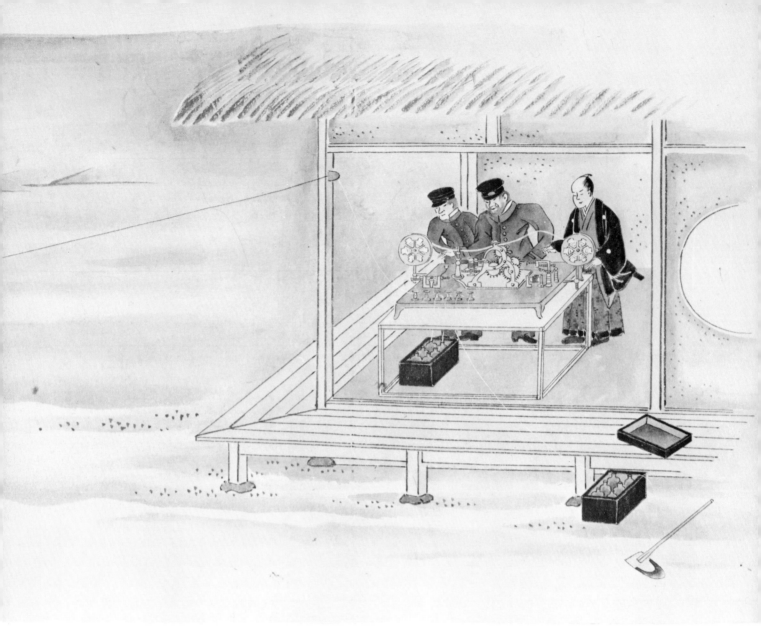

The telegraph brought by the Americans

learned how to set it up from Samuel Morse, the inventor.
Japanese stood in line for hours in order to send messages.
Some of them raced from one end of the line to the other,
as fast as they could, astonished to discover that a telegraph
message traveled more quickly than they could run.

A miniature railroad was the hit of the show. It consisted
of a toy-size engine, tender, and passenger cars designed to
run 350 feet around a circular track 18 inches wide. It was
so small that a person had to sit on top in order to drive it.
Samurai took turns whirling around at the rate of twenty
miles per hour, their loose robes flying in the wind as they

THE RETURN OF THE BARBARIANS

clung to the roof. They laughed and behaved as though they were riding a roller coaster.

American clothing was another source of fascination. Japanese tagged after sailors and officers in order to have a close-up look at their strange costumes. Many of them were so overcome by curiosity that they could not resist touching the uniformed men. They were allowed to finger hats, jackets, pants, and shoes. Some even put their hands inside pockets, much to the amusement of the Americans. Buttons intrigued them particularly, because the Japanese used various types of cords and strings to fasten their own clothing. Button collecting became a new hobby, and people gladly offered food or trinkets in exchange for the treasured mementos.

The exhibition of gifts was as much fun as any country fair or a carnival could be. Sailors and samurai had a jolly time, despite the many spies on the lookout for natives who acted *too* friendly.

Gifts marked "To the Emperor" and "To the Empress"

The train was toy-sized, as in the top drawing. Below we see a representation by Hiroshige III, which became popular as a souvenir after the Americans had departed.

were sent to Edo and kept by the new Shogun. The descendent of the sun goddess never received the telescope, champagne, steam engine, and telegraph sets intended for him. Nor were the soaps, perfumes, and the embroidered dress meant for his wife ever delivered to the royal palace at Kyoto.

Gifts for the Americans

The Japanese reciprocated by inviting the Commodore and his officers to receive presents from the Emperor. Gifts were heaped on tables, benches, and even on the floor of the Treaty House. Commissioner Hayashi read aloud, in Japanese, the list of presents and the names of the persons to whom they were to be given. His words were translated into Dutch, then into English.

There were scrolls, lacquer boxes and trays, porcelain tea sets, bamboo stands, silks, garments, dolls, jars of soy sauce, swords, umbrellas, and hundreds of unusual seashells. Three spaniels, a breed of dog restricted to the emperor and the shogun, were intended for the Commodore and the President of the United States. (See Appendix D.)

Many Americans, including the Commodore, were disappointed in the quality of the gifts. "A poor display, not worth over a thousand dollars, some thought," Lieutenant Preble noted in his diary.[1] The Americans undervalued the finely woven silks, the artistic lacquerware, the delicately light porcelain, and the incomparably beautiful, sharp swords. In fact, because he was a natural history buff, Perry was most impressed with the seashells.

After seeing the display of gifts, the Americans were invited outside to see a very special present from the Emperor to the entire crew—200 bales of rice, each weighing between 100 and 150 pounds. Seated near these bales, they watched a procession of about fifty huge sumo wrestlers, who were incredibly fat, muscular giants. The Americans had never seen men as fleshy and massive as these athletes, who had been fed special diets so that each weighed between 250 and 400 pounds. Lieutenant Preble was shocked because "they were entirely naked except that they wore a stout silken girdle about their loins concealing what modesty should not expose."[2]

Mammoth men were (and still are) sports stars of Japan. Sumo wrestlers used to be pampered favorites of daimyos, who kept them for their own private amusement and occasionally showed them off for public entertainment. They had been brought from Edo for the occasion. A wrestler named

Shunsho's *Portrait of Two Wrestlers*

Koyanagi, called "the bully of the capital," was presented to Perry by the commissioners, who urged the Commodore to feel the sumo champion's bulging muscles and to "punch him in the paunch."[3] He gripped Koyanagi's huge arm, then felt the neck, which, he noted, was creased like that of a prize ox. Officers also examined the wrestler, and when they uttered exclamations of disbelief, he answered with an appreciative grunt.

Marines examine a sumo wrestler on March 24, 1854.

At a given signal, each of these strong men seized two bales of rice and carried them above their heads with apparent ease. One held a sack with his teeth. Another repeatedly turned somersaults as he held on to his bales. The wrestlers brought the rice to the edge of the water. Later the sailors

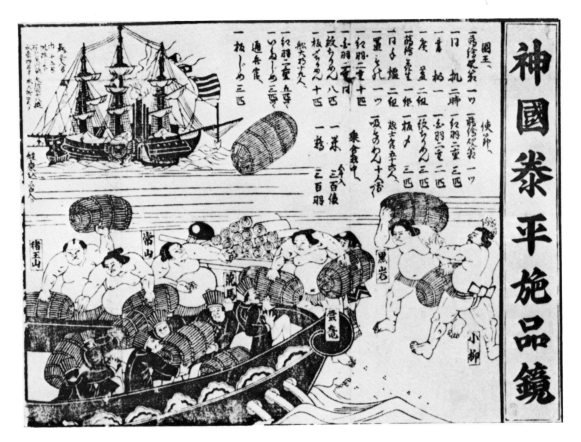

Sumo wrestlers easily carry 150 pound rice bales.

huffed and puffed, lifting the bales into their boats and unloading them.

The Americans were then escorted to the rear of the Treaty House to watch sumo wrestling matches. As the athletic giants tussled, the audience was served a meal of eggs, shrimps, lobsters, oysters, and a broth that Preble suspected was "a cup of raw fish or snake soup." (Preble also thought that drinking saki was "detestable." Nevertheless, "following the custom of the country," the lieutenant pocketed leftovers.)[4]

The wrestling matches were fascinating. The athletes had servants who helped them dress and undress. The contenders paraded around a small circular arena that had been prepared for the sport. At a signal given by an elaborately gowned referee, two sumo wrestlers entered the ring, stretched their legs, stamped about, glared at each other, and scattered fists full of salt about the ring. Salt, a symbol of purity, was also rubbed on their bodies. Crouched like football linemen, with fists touching the ground, they suddenly slammed together, each trying to heave the other to the floor or out of the ring. They yelled and screeched when they fought, but as soon as a contestant won, both became quiet and courteous. The winner bowed to the loser and politely helped his downed opponent to his feet. Each contest took but a few minutes, and the sport ended when all athletes had wrestled.

After this Perry ordered a detachment of marines to put on an exhibition drill that would contrast with the "brutal performance" of "monsters" whose "animal natures had been carefully developed."[5] (One wonders how the Commodore would have described the bloody bare-knuckled boxing matches of one hundred or more rounds that were being staged in America at that time.)

Interpreter Williams wrote that it was quite a day. "A junction of East and West . . . epaulettes and uniforms, shaven pates and nightgowns, soldiers with muskets and drilling in close array, soldiers with petticoats, sandals, two swords . . . exhibiting the difference between our civilization and usages and those of this secluded, pagan people."[6]

12 • THE GRAND BANQUET

BEFORE GOING BACK TO THE SHIP the Commodore invited the commissioners and their retinue to dine aboard the *Powhatan*. [1]

The Japanese first visited the *Macedonian* and were ushered all over the ship. Once again, their intense curiosity amused the crew, for they examined every inch of the vessel and even stuck their heads into the mouths of cannons. The sailors put on a fire drill during which they threw buckets of water and pumped streams of it at imaginary fires. The sailors also amused their guests by firing guns and by demonstrating how they prepared to board an enemy ship and how they were organized to repel attackers. This show of power was not lost on the Japanese. Long before this day many thought that a treaty with the Americans offered their only chance of peaceful survival. [2]

When they boarded the *Powhatan* they were shown the steamship's massive machinery before being seated for a feast. Because Japanese etiquette would not allow the commissioners to sit at the same table as their subordinates, the Commodore arranged two banquets: one in his cabin, for dignitaries, the other on quarterdeck for their retainers.

Once again the Commodore put on a good show. He believed that diplomacy through dining was important, and

OVERLEAF:
The grand
dinner on deck

therefore a French chef was an essential member of his staff. Perry wrote, "I spared no pains in providing most bountifully, being desirous of giving them some idea of American hospitality in comparison with their portions of fish soup. My Paris cook labored for a week, night and day, in getting up a variety of ornamental dishes."[3] The menu included soups, fish, beef, fowl, pickles, pies, and fruits. Each commissioner was presented with a cake decorated with his own flag and coat of arms.

A variety of wines and liqueurs inspired toasts to the Commodore, the commissioners, the President, and more and more frequently as they filled their glasses, to the ladies of Japan and America. Preble noted that "A most laughable scene was seeing one of our officers toasting the Japs who looked like two bundles of clothes, skewered by two swords."[4]

Instructed to encourage guests to eat and drink as much as possible, Preble plied the Japanese on deck with wines, whiskey, and punch. When there was no more, he "gave them a mixture of catsup and vinegar, which they seemed to relish with equal gusto."[5]

When the band played, several started shuffling and dancing, and to encourage them in the gaiety, American officers danced with them. What a sight! "The bald-pated bundles of clothes [Samurai]—and Doctors, Pursers, Lieutenants and Captains all jumping up and down to music."[6] One elderly samurai was seen on the hurricane deck learning the polka from a midshipman.

Each guest was encouraged to take home leftovers. In addition to pieces of pie, beef, and chicken, one fellow emptied a saltcellar, and another poured sugar into a paper handkerchief that he had cleverly folded into an envelope.

After dinner the commissioners joined the others on deck. All the Japanese were given front-row seats for a minstrel show, staged by American sailors. Programs, which had been

A minstrel show

printed on board ship, were distributed so that the audience would know that the theatrical performance was done by the Japanese Minstrels. They were amused by the blackened faces, banjos, tamborines, and silly dancing. They certainly could not understand dialogue, and they knew nothing about Africans who had been brought to America as slaves.

When it was time to leave, a commissioner who was a bit tipsy but brimming with goodwill said, "Japan and America, all the same heart." He hugged the Commodore so hard that Perry's new epaulettes were crushed. Perry did not mind the hug. "Oh," he said to his officers, "if they will only sign the Treaty he may kiss me."[7]

13 • THE TREATY

THE CREW WAS RESTLESS AND BORED while waiting around for a treaty to be signed. Many of the men were disappointed because the Land of the Rising Sun was not glistening with riches. They were exhilarated, however, when a report came from the *Saratoga*'s galley. The chef had found particles of gold inside the gizzards of ducks that had been slaughtered for dinner. One nugget was as large as a pea. A land where poultry fed upon gold! What fabulous prospects for fortune hunters! Japan may prove to be a treasure island, after all. But the dreams of wealth were short-lived. The purser on the *Saratoga* submitted the metal to a test and found that it was only copper.

On March 31, the day after the golden gizzard fiasco, Perry received his greatest treasure—a treaty with Japan. The Commodore went to the Treaty House in order to receive copies of the Treaty of Kanagawa in four languages: English, Dutch, Japanese, and Chinese. It provided for:

- Peace and friendship between the United States of America and the Empire of Japan.
- The opening of two ports to American ships: Shimoda and Hakodate.

- Assistance for any American ships that are wrecked on the Japanese coast and protection of shipwrecked persons.
- Assurance that shipwrecked men and other U.S. citizens would not be confined and controlled like the Dutch who were at Nagasaki.
- U.S. consuls or agents would be allowed to reside in Shimoda "provided that either of the two governments deem such arrangements necessary."
- Japanese officers would supply ships with coal, water, and other necessary provisions.
- *Most favored nation clause:* The United States would receive all privileges that other nations may receive in the future.
- The Treaty "is to be ratified and approved by the President of the United States, by and with the advice and consent of the Senate thereof, and by the august Sovereign of Japan, and the ratification shall be exchanged within eighteen months . . . or sooner." (See Appendix E.)

The treaty was the result of weeks of tiresome talks. After the Japanese conceded the ports of Shimoda and Hakodate, they expected to be able to confine Americans at these villages. Then they compromised by allowing Americans to travel seven *ri* (about seventeen miles) in any direction out of town.

The prospect of American consuls living in Japan was another subject of debate. Perry firmly insisted that consuls must be received—unless the Japanese wanted an American warship constantly docked at one of their ports. The Commodore finally stipulated that only one consul would be sent to reside in Shimoda, but not until eighteen months had passed.

The Japanese commissioners felt they had "saved face" and deluded themselves into believing that they had not conceded anything of great importance. They had not named any major ports: Shimoda and Hakodate were villages remote from the important cities of Osaka and Edo. They had prevented Perry from entering Edo. They had shielded the Shogun and the Emperor. They had maintained peace. The prospect of a consul coming from the United States seemed unlikely, for although the American text of the treaty stated that either of the two governments had to "deem such arrangement necessary," the Japanese text read that *both* Japanese and American governments must deem such arrangements *unavoidable*. (Two years later when consul Townsend Harris arrived in Shimoda, the authorities told him to leave. They were appalled that he established a consulate without the Shogun's consent.)

Perry was pleased with the treaty, for although it was not a trade agreement, it did guarantee protection of castaways, and it specified two ports that would supply provisions for Yankee whalers, warships, and merchant vessels. He had a foot in the door and in the future it would not be difficult to open up a wide entrance to this closed-in country. The isolated Empire of Japan would soon join the society of world nations.

On March 31, 1854, the treaty was signed by the Commodore as representative of the U.S. government and by four commissioners in the name of the Emperor. The Emperor eventually received a copy, with unrealistic assurances from the Shogun's emissaries that the document was of no importance.

After the signing Perry presented an American flag to the chief commissioner "to evidence our intention never to oppose your country."[1] Then the Japanese invited the Americans to a banquet.

A Japanese Feast

All sat down to a feast consisting of thick soups and stews of fish, plates of crayfish, shrimps, fried fish, seaweed jelly,

Hideki's sketch of the Japanese feast for the Americans

puddings, cakes, and countless cups of rice saki, which were needed for the toasts. The courses were cooked and presented artistically, but the food was not for the Yankee palate. Midshipman Edward McCauley declared that he could detect "the flavor of cat, dog, rat, and snake."[2] Perry, more subtle in his remarks, wrote that the dinner "left an unfavorable impression on their skill of cookery."[3]

The Americans, however, marveled at the courtesy and politeness of their hosts and to please them, many adopted the Japanese custom of wrapping leftovers and taking food back to their ships.

The Japanese were appalled by the Americans' table manners, which they called "disgusting." The men were too informal, their conversation was too loud, and their table manners were messy. (They couldn't handle chopsticks.) But the banquet was fun, and everyone was friendly.

It is remarkable that people in the land of the Shogun could be so gracious and hospitable to unwanted visitors from the Black Ships and that the Americans could overcome their prejudice against a "different" people and enjoy their company.

A finished Hideki painting of the same feast

THE RETURN OF THE BARBARIANS

14 • EXCURSIONS ON LAND AND SEA

AFTER THE TREATY WAS SIGNED, the Commodore and members of his staff were invited to tour nearby villages. Perry was annoyed when he realized that as soon as he approached a settlement the streets were practically deserted and the women were ordered indoors. When he mentioned his displeasure, Yenosuke, his escort and interpreter, apologized by saying that the ladies were too modest to be seen by strangers. Perry refused to believe this. Yenosuke then promised that at the next village women would be told not to avoid the foreigners. After that, crowds including females filled the streets, happy to gawk at the strange-looking Americans.

Perry and his escorts were entertained at the home of a village mayor, where they were served the traditional tea, cakes, and saki. Barefoot women wearing something that the Commodore thought looked more like nightgowns than dresses waited on them. The women remained on their knees crawling from one guest to another and bowing their heads to the floor as they offered refreshments. Perry was delighted with the hospitality, but he did not appreciate the ladies' smiles. Their gums and teeth were painted black, a custom that had been fashionable for a thousand years. Not only married women, but also courtiers blackened their teeth for beauty's sake. The sailors called the black-teethed ladies "walking ink bottles."[1]

Dr. James Morrow

Other members of the American squadron were allowed to take walks around Yokohama. Interpreter Williams accompanied his close friend Dr. James Morrow, the official "agriculturalist" for the Perry Expedition. The men meandered through the countryside collecting flowers and plants. They also waded along the shore for shelled creatures and seaweeds. When Williams encountered near-naked fishermen digging for clams, he was shocked by their nudity and declared that these heathens needed "the gospel of purity and love."[2]

A few of the sailors on shore leave used white paint to scrawl their names on rocks. The graffiti caused a great deal of commotion when it was discovered. The Japanese did not know what the strange signs meant. One man, posing as a scholar, announced that the writing was a poem to nature written in ancient Chinese hieroglyphics. Another self-appointed wise man deciphered the letters as pictographs that said "In the Year of the First Tiger [1854] since it was his birthday he could not but stop. King Hatan [the American ruler] therefore gave up commencing war on that day."[3]

A Birthday Cruise

In the Year of the First Tiger (1854) on his sixtieth birthday (April 10), Commodore Perry determined to go as near to Edo as the depth of water would allow. The steamships *Powhatan* and *Mississippi* set sail. Japanese interpreters who had come aboard to say goodbye went into a panic. They begged Perry not to approach the capital city. His Black Ships would create chaos in Edo, and as a result the interpreters and commissioners would suffer disgrace. All of them would be obligated to commit suicide.

As the ships steamed ahead, Yenosuke exclaimed that when a planned salute was fired off Edo he would throw himself into a cannon's mouth. Another interpreter handed his robe and long sword to one of the crew, saying that he had no further use for them. With great composure, he prepared to disembowel himself with his short sword. This was to be done at the very moment an anchor was lowered.

Perry ordered his ships to turn back, for "though somewhat incredulous as to the necessity of their performing hara-kiri on themselves," he wrote, "I thought it better policy not to proceed."[4] The ships sailed near Edo, and with the aid of a telescope Perry could see its rooftops and its canvas "dungaree forts." The Japanese interpreters were so relieved that they were able to enjoy a luncheon party in the Commodore's cabin.

Although he never entered Edo, Perry was satisfied with his excursion. He concluded that "the city of Edo can be destroyed by a few steamers of very light draft, and carrying guns of the heaviest caliber."[5] It was a happy birthday, with no hara-kiri to mar the occasion.

15 • SHORE LEAVE

Shore leave

EIGHT DAYS AFTER HIS CRUISE toward Edo the Commodore decided to visit Shimoda and Hakodate, the ports specified in the treaty.

Shimoda

The fishing village of Shimoda was isolated from the rest of the country by rugged mountains. From the Japanese point of view Shimoda was a perfect port for foreigners, just because it was remote. It was situated at the tip of the fifty-mile-long peninsula of Izu. At one time Japanese rulers used Izu for exiles.

Even though Shimoda was hemmed in by mountains, Perry was pleased because its harbor had room for many ships. The Commodore was overwhelmed by its beauty and he was very impressed by the streets' cleanliness. The village had gutters and sewers. Most Western cities did not have adequate sanitation systems at that time. "Shimoda shows an advanced state of civilization," Perry wrote, "much beyond our own boasted progress in the attention to . . . cleanliness and healthfulness."[1]

The Commodore and his officers were housed in a Bud-

Landing at Shimoda, June 8, 1854

dhist temple that they furnished with chairs, tables, and bedding from the ships. Enlisted men, who occupied a nearby temple, sat and slept on spotlessly clean floor mats laid out for them by Japanese servants.

Everyone looked forward to touring this exotic port, but the villagers were terrified. They were afraid of the long-nosed aliens. Some frightened families hid in lofts that had been built for storage. Others guarded their cattle because they had heard that the Americans ate beef. (Until the 1870s Japanese used cattle solely for farm work; never for food.) Streets were deserted, shops were closed, and spies followed the men from the Black Ships.

The Commodore complained to officials. After that, crowds filled the streets, stores opened, and households enter-

The temple grounds at Shimoda

tained the foreigners. Some women, overcoming their distaste for moustaches and curly hair, accompanied sailors.

The Americans quickly became objects of friendly curiosity. People in the street were not shy about fingering their buttons, uniforms, and weapons. The navy men were accustomed to the people's insatiable curiosity and enjoyed this familiarity. Lieutenant Preble was sensational. He astonished villagers by taking out his false teeth. Preble was amused by their reaction. He was sure his audience believed that all Americans could carry their teeth in their pockets.

Visiting a bathhouse proved to be a popular pastime. The Americans gawked at men and women who bathed together "in a state of absolute nudity, not having even Adam's fig leaf and all scrubbing themselves assiduously without regard to each other."[2] Perry was shocked that they were "uncon-

THE RETURN OF THE BARBARIANS

scious of their nudity."[3] The Japanese were amused and incredulous that a common bathhouse could prove to be such an attraction.

Dancing

The mayor of Shimoda arranged for a daily bazaar so that the Americans could conveniently shop for souvenirs. Preble griped because the Commodore and his officers had first pick and grabbed the best.

Some sailors became drunk and disorderly. Two of them pulled out the spigot from a barrel of saki, let it flow on the shop's floor, then scuffled with the shopkeeper. The Commodore was furious, and the culprits were locked up on board ship.

The people of Shimoda made numerous sketches of the foreigners. As a result, we have many illustrations depicting sailors' behavior—and misbehavior. The Americans took photographs of Japanese women. (Town officials allowed geisha girls to pose for them.) The villagers were fascinated. They had never seen cameras before, and they called the photographs "magic mirrors." However, a few superstitious people decided that a camera was a "murder box" intended to capture a person's image in order to destroy that person. They urged everyone to avoid the daguerreotype equipment.

About to be photographed

One day the Americans saw two Japanese prisoners who were locked in a small cage. They were being carried through the streets of Shimoda. (Yoshida Shoin, the famous revolutionary mentioned in Chapter 8, page 56, and another liberal named Kaneko, were these caged prisoners.) The men had tried to defect to the United States. They had rowed out to the *Mississippi* and asked to be taken to America. The Commodore refused because the men had not received their government's permission. He would not chance infuriating officials who had finally agreed to cooperate with him, but Perry was appalled at their plight. The men were subsequently imprisoned in Edo.[4]

Botanist Morrow and his best friend, interpreter Williams, took advantage of the ruling that allowed them to wander out of town. They took daily walks in the hills gathering plants, visiting blacksmiths, observing silkworm cultivation, watching weavers, and chatting with farmers. They marveled at Japan's advanced irrigation system, and they swapped American seeds for Japanese seeds that they brought back to the United States.

Hakodate

Hakodate was a distant outpost in Hokkaido, the northernmost of the four main islands of Japan. It was bleak, sparsely inhabited, and valuable primarily for whalers. Because of the treaty they could come here when they needed provisions or a stopover for repairs and recreation.

As soon as the Americans landed alarm gongs were sounded and villagers were driven indoors by policemen armed with whips. The daimyo of the district forbade citizens to even *look* at the Black Ships, and the Americans were ordered to leave at once.

The Commodore presented a copy of the Treaty of Kanagawa to officials, who claimed that they knew nothing about the agreement. They were not telling the truth, because their daimyo had been told by the Shogun's messengers to expect the Americans. They were also warned that the foreigners loved liquor and ladies, and might be unruly.

With the help of seventy of the daimyo's retainers, women and children were shipped out of Hakodate and housed with relatives and friends in the mountains. Women who remained home were ordered to hide behind locked doors. Official instructions even specified that they must paste cracks in houses with paper so that sailors would not be able to peek in at them. (Lieutenant Preble noticed tiny

The conference room at Hakodate   Hunting

holes torn in paper windows, probably made by females curious to see the strange looking foreigners.) In addition, there were orders to hide saki and close all shops.

Once again, the Commodore complained, and the officials complied with Perry's demand that shops be opened and his men be greeted in a friendly manner. However, no women were allowed to mingle with the Americans.

Despite the absence of female company, the men had a great time. Hunting game proved to be fun, and the fishing was fantastic. The Japanese enjoyed a brisk business when the foreigners jammed into shops to buy plaided silks, pots, and

Fishing at Hakodate

assorted souvenirs. Some sailors brought dogs and cats back to the ships.

Merchants were shocked because the Americans entered shops with their boots on and were boisterous. "Going thus to a store to buy is not the way of a samurai."[5]

After the port was surveyed Perry entertained the daimyo's retainers with supper and a minstrel show aboard ship. The audience seemed amused, and Perry was satisfied that he was leaving them with a good impression.

As a parting gift the daimyo's men presented the Commodore with a block of granite for the Washington Monument. They wished to honor the name of the only American "king" they had ever heard of.

THE RETURN OF THE BARBARIANS

16 • IN THE WAKE OF THE BLACK SHIPS

By COINCIDENCE, while Perry was still in Japan an American whaling ship anchored near his fleet. The *Eliza F. Mason* arrived at Hakodate in May 1854, twenty-one months after leaving New Bedford, Massachusetts. He never would have dared to land, but the presence of Yankee warships made Captain Jernegan of the whaler sufficiently comfortable to come ashore with his nine-year-old son and his wife Abigail. She was the first foreign female the Japanese had ever seen, and she created a sensation when she entered the village. Abigail permitted some of the women to lift her voluminous skirts in order to examine her shoes and peek at her pantaloons. She was enchanted by their interest in her and praised their gentle manners. She stayed overnight in Hakodate with her husband and son.

When the Jernegans went back to their ship the following day, the Japanese delivered a beautifully wrapped package that contained an item Abigail had left behind. It was a common pin!

Only fifteen days after Commodore Perry left Japan, the first American tourists arrived. The *Lady Pierce,* a private yacht owned by a Connecticut man, Silas E. Burrows, entered the Bay of Edo on July 11, 1854. Burrows used the excuse of returning a Japanese castaway for an adventure into

An unknown Japanese
artist's portrait of
Americans in Nagasaki,
1860

the Forbidden Land. He did not know that Perry had signed
the Treaty of Kanagawa, but as a result of that treaty the
Yankees were welcome visitors.

A fleet of Japanese fishermen cheered as the yacht approached the shore. Visitors from Uraga brought gifts of
silks, porcelains, and lacquerware when they crowded on
board. Burrows treated them to a boat tour and refreshments.
Local officials enjoyed the hospitality but explained that a
recent treaty specified Shimoda and Hakodate as the sole
ports open to Americans.

Burrows landed at Shimoda, where he returned the castaway. He and his crew remained there for a week, going
ashore every day to see the sights. They distributed otter
skins and gold coins that had been specially minted for them
in San Francisco. However, after an interpreter discovered

"Liberty" stamped on each coin, the gold pieces were collected and returned to Burrows.

Nevertheless, Burrows praised the politeness of the natives and was pleased to report that the Japanese told him that they greatly admired Commodore Perry and his officers!

Soon after news of the Treaty of Kanagawa was published in Hawaiian newspapers, a group of American merchants chartered a schooner, the *Caroline E. Foote*. They wanted to set up a supply depot and import-export offices in Japan. Using sailing directions that were published by Commodore Perry, they arrived at Shimoda in March 1855.

The town had been hit by an earthquake and tidal waves in December 1854. All but sixteen Shimoda buildings had

Mr. and Mrs. Reed, their five year old daughter, and Mrs. Worth, wife of the captain of the *Carolyn E. Foote*

been destroyed, and hundreds of people had drowned. The village was being hastily rebuilt, possibly because the government feared that if Shimoda wasn't reconstructed quickly the Americans might demand another port in its place. (Many Japanese were positive that the earthquake was a sign that the gods were angry.)

Six Yankee merchants, three wives, and two children from the *Foote* were housed in a temple. Shortly after they moved in, a Japanese woman who had followed them accepted an invitation to come inside. One of the American ladies allowed her to try on Western clothing. The villager dressed herself up and whitened her face with flour so that her complexion would look "American." When she saw herself in the mirror, she clapped her hands and laughed at her image. Unfortunately, a policeman was spying. He entered the temple, chased her out by smacking her with his bamboo cane, and put her in jail.

The passengers of the *Foote* became known as "American Pioneers." Although they stayed in Shimoda almost three months, they were unable to establish a trading post there. They left for Hakodate in June 1855, where they also failed. So they set sail for San Francisco, convinced that Japan would never be a land of commercial opportunity.

Before the American Pioneers left Japan, they met Russians who had been stranded in Shimoda after their ship was destroyed by the 1854 tidal wave. They also met the crews of one French warship, three British men of war, and countless U.S. Navy ships. All had docked and disembarked at Shimoda. Within two years after the American treaty, Britain, Russia, and Holland had made treaties with Japan similar to the one Perry had negotiated. Foreigners became commonplace on the sacred soil of the Land of the Rising Sun.[1]

Artist Yoshikazu's view of Americans touring Yokahama

AFTERWORD

The First American Consul

IN 1856, TWO YEARS after Perry's Japan expeditions, Townsend Harris arrived at Shimoda. As first consul general from the United States, he had two aims: to establish a consulate and to negotiate a trade treaty.

The Japanese were dismayed by his presence, and they begged him to leave. When he refused, they allowed him to settle in one of the temples. Spies followed him everywhere, the natives snubbed him, and for sixteen months he felt isolated. His main companion was a Dutch secretary-interpreter he had brought with him.

Stubborn and courageous—without Perry's big guns to back him up—Harris used clever diplomacy to gain his objectives. He warned officials that the British were probably scheming to attack Japan, and he constantly referred to the successful battles the British and French were waging in China at that time. Surely it was preferable to yield to the peaceful requests of a consul rather than to an armed fleet of European aggressors!

Harris had in his possession a letter from President Franklin Pierce requesting a trade agreement between the United States and Japan. The Consul insisted upon going to Edo to see the Shogun. In order to induce government advisers to comply with his wishes, Harris offered to reveal a plot hatched by the British against Japan. (He probably referred to the English fleet at Hong Kong that *may* have schemed to sail to the Land of the Shogun.)

A year after his arrival in Shimoda, Harris was invited to Edo to see the Shogun. Having learned from Perry the importance of pomp and ceremony, he made elaborate preparations for the great event. Forty porters, twelve guardsmen, two standard bearers, two shoe and fan bearers, and two grooms were part of a retinue of 350 men. All except the porters wore silk dresses embroidered with the American coat of arms (the eagle, arrows, olive branch, and motto *E pluribus unum*). "Daimyo" Harris was carried in a custom-made palanquin, big enough for him to stretch out his legs. It was an elaborate cage suspended from the ground by two poles, which twelve bearers carried on their shoulders. The usual palanquin was small enough for two or four bearers.

In December 1857, the American Consul General had an audience with Shogun Iesada. Although everyone else was down on his knees, Harris stood upright in the presence of the "Tycoon" (Harris's name for the Shogun). He presented the President's letter and was informed that the Shogun was pleased with its contents.

However, Harris was not able to negotiate a treaty overnight. There were innumerable meetings with the Shogun's adviser. By the end of February 1858, a Treaty of Amity and Commerce was drawn up. It permitted full trade, authorized an American representative to live in Edo, and opened additional ports. The treaty was signed by a special assistant to the Shogun, who believed it was in the best interests of Japan. Therefore, he was "determined to accept suffering and punishment for concluding [the treaty] without the Emperor's sanction."[1]

The Fall of the Shogun

The treaty caused a critical rift between supporters of the Emperor and followers of the Shogun. Emperor Komei announced that the treaty was "a blemish on this country which was created and protected by deities. . . . Since this treaty spells the doom of our nation I cannot in any way sanction it."[2]

Fanatics wanted all foreigners thrown out immediately. On the other hand, many scholars insisted that the isolation policy was out of date and could result in war. Japan needed Western culture and commerce to survive as an independent nation.

Emperor Meiji entering Edo after leaving Kyoto.

Activists who opposed shoguns became more and influential. In 1867 the reigning Shogun Keiki resigned. He hoped that by stepping down from office he would unite the country. A year later the fifteen-year-old Emperor was declared the true divine ruler. In 1868 Emperor Meiji's reign began. He left the imperial grounds in Kyoto and moved to establish his palace at Edo. Edo was renamed Tokyo, which means "Eastern capital."

Emperor Meiji's rule brought Japan out of the feudal past and into the modern industrial world. Scholars were sent abroad to study, and foreign advisers were welcome. Within five years all castes were outlawed. Daimyos surrendered lands and privileges they had enjoyed for a thousand years.

Emperor Meiji

They turned their estates over to the Emperor, who awarded them generous pensions as compensation. The samurai class was abolished. Laws forbade the traditional warriors from wearing swords. Even their top-knot hairdos were prohibited. The government awarded them modest pensions. Surprisingly, they transferred their loyalty from their daimyos to the Emperor with little protest.

For the first time in centuries people were able to choose the type of work they wished to do. They could live wherever they wished, and there were no longer set rules about the types of homes, possessions, and clothing they were allowed. The Emperor set a new style: After 1872 he wore Western clothing.

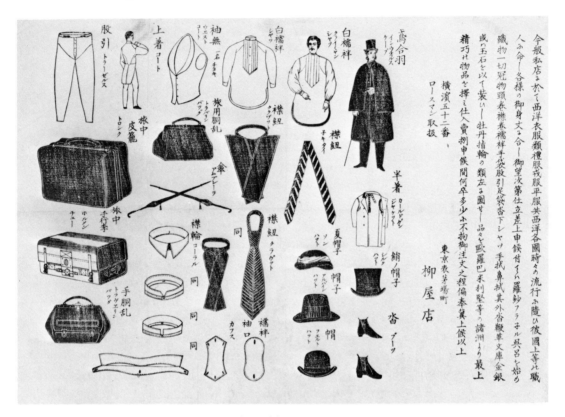

This Japanese chart explains how to dress like a Westerner.

The jump from feudalism to a modern industrial society took place with astounding speed and ease. Historians still marvel at the quick change that took place without foreign or civil war.

Commodore Perry broke down barriers that separated Japan from the rest of the world. Today the Japanese celebrate his expeditions with annual Black Ships festivals. At Shimoda, where feudal warriors once mobilized against the Yankee barbarians, parades, speeches, and music honor Perry

北亞墨利加人物

ペルリ像

in May. At Kanagawa, where the treaty was signed, people enjoy their Black Ships festival in July. They commemorate the Commodore who brought them peacefully into a world that never would have permitted them to continue their isolation.

Commodore Perry lived in Newport, Rhode Island, which celebrates a Black Ships festival in July. In Perry's honor, Newport has become Shimoda's sister city.

APPENDICES

APPENDIX A

Letter of the President of the United States to the Emperor of Japan

Great and Good Friend!

I send you this public letter by Commodore Matthew C. Perry, an officer of highest rank in the Navy of the United States, and commander of the squadron now visiting Your Imperial Majesty's dominions.

I have directed Commodore Perry to assure Your Imperial Majesty that I entertain the kindest feelings toward Your Majesty's person and government, and that I have no other object in sending him to Japan but to propose to Your Imperial Majesty that the United States and Japan should live in friendship and have commercial intercourse with each other.

The constitution and laws of the United States forbid all interference with the religious or political concerns of other nations. I have particularly charged Commodore Perry to abstain from every act which could possibly disturb the tranquillity of Your Imperial Majesty's dominions.

The United States of America reach from ocean to ocean, and our territory of Oregon and state of California lie directly opposite to the dominions of Your Imperial Majesty. Our steamships can go from California to Japan in eighteen days.

Our great state of California produces about sixty millions of dollars in gold every year, besides silver, quicksilver, precious stones, and many other valuable articles. Japan is also a rich and fertile country and produces many very valuable articles. Your Imperial Majesty's subjects are skilled in many of the arts. I am desirous that our two countries should trade with each other for the benefit both of Japan and the United States.

We know that the ancient laws of Your Imperial Majesty's government do not allow of foreign trade except with the Dutch. But as the state of the world changes, and new governments are formed, it seems to be wise from time to time to make new laws. There was a time when the ancient laws of Your Imperial Majesty's government were first made.

About the same time America, which is sometimes called the New World, was first discovered and settled by the Europeans. For a long time there were but a few people, and they were poor. They have now become quite numerous; their commerce is very extensive; and they think that if Your Imperial Majesty were so far to change the ancient laws as to allow a free trade between the two countries, it would be extremely beneficial to both.

If Your Imperial Majesty is not satisfied that it would be safe, altogether, to abrogate the ancient laws which forbid foreign trade, they might be suspended for five or ten years, so as to try the experiment. If it does not prove as beneficial as was hoped, the ancient laws can be restored. The United States often limits its treaties with foreign states to a few years, and then renews them or not, as they please.

I have directed Commodore Perry to mention another thing to Your Imperial Majesty. Many of our ships pass every year from California to China, and great numbers of our people pursue the whale fishery near the shores of Japan. It sometimes happens in stormy weather that one of our ships is wrecked on Your Imperial Majesty's shores. In all such cases we ask and expect that our unfortunate people should be treated with kindness, and that their property should be protected till we can send a vessel and bring them away. We are very much in earnest in this.

Commodore Perry is also directed by me to represent to Your Imperial Majesty that we understand that there is a great abundance of coal and provisions in the empire of Japan. Our steamships, in crossing the great ocean, burn a great deal of coal, and it is not convenient to bring it all the way from America. We wish that our steamships and other vessels should be allowed to stop in Japan and supply themselves with coal, provisions, and water. They will pay for them in money, or anything else Your Imperial Majesty's subjects may prefer, and we request Your Imperial Majesty to appoint a convenient port in the southern part of the empire where our vessels may stop for this purpose. We are very desirous of this.

These are the only objects for which I have sent Commodore Perry with a powerful squadron to pay a visit to Your Imperial Majesty's renowned city of Edo: friendship, commerce, a supply of coal, and provisions and protection for our shipwrecked people.

We have directed Commodore Perry to beg Your Imperial Majesty's acceptance of a few presents. They are of no great value in themselves, but some of them may serve as specimens of the articles manufactured in the United States, and they are intended as tokens of our sincere and respectful friendship.

May the Almighty have Your Imperial Majesty in his great and holy keeping!

In witness whereof I have caused the great seal of the United States to be hereunto affixed, and have subscribed the same with my name, at the city of Washington in America, the seal of my government, on the thirteenth day of the month of November, in the year one thousand eight hundred and fifty-two.

Your good friend,
MILLARD FILLMORE

By the President
EDWARD EVERETT
SECRETARY OF STATE

APPENDIX B

Translation of Answer to the President's Letter, Signed by Yenosuke

The return of Your Excellency as Ambassador of the United States to this Empire has been expected according to the letter of his majesty the President, which your excellency delivered last year to his majesty the Emperor of this nation. It is quite impossible to give satisfactory answers at once to all the proposals of your government.

Although a change is most positively forbidden by the laws of our imperial ancestors, for us to continue attached to ancient laws seems to misunderstand the spirit of the age. Nevertheless we are governed now by imperative necessity. At the visit of your excellency to this Empire last year, his majesty the former Emperor was sick and is now dead. Subsequently his majesty the present Emperor ascended the throne. The many occupations in consequence thereof are not yet finished and there is no time to settle other business thoroughly. Moreover his majesty the new Emperor at his succession to the throne promised the princes and high officers of the empire to observe the laws; it is therefore evident that he cannot now bring about any alterations in the ancient laws.

Last autumn at the departure of the Dutch ship, the superintendent of the Dutch trade in Japan was requested to inform your government of this event, and we have been informed in writing that he did so.

The Russian Ambassador arrived recently at Nagasaki to communicate a wish of his government. He has since left the said place because no answer would be given to whatever nation that might communicate similar wishes. We recognize necessity, however, and shall entirely comply with the proposals of your government concerning coal, wood, water, provisions, and the saving of ships and their crews in distress. After being informed which harbor your excellency selects, that harbor shall be prepared, which preparation it is estimated will take about five years. Meanwhile commencement can be made with the coal at Nagasaki, by the first month of the next Japanese year (16 February 1855).

Having no precedent with respect to coal, we request your excellency to furnish us with an estimate, and upon due consideration this will be complied with if not in opposition to our laws. What do you mean by provisions, and how much coal will be required?

Finally, anything ships may be in want of that can be furnished from the production of this Empire shall be supplied; the prices of merchandise and articles of barter to be fixed by Kahei Kurokawa and Einosuke Moriyama. After settling the points beforementioned, the treaty can be concluded and signed at the next interview.

APPENDIX C

Some of the American Presents for the Japanese[1]

FOR THE EMPEROR

Miniature steam engine, ¼ size, with track, tender, and car.

2 telegraph sets, with batteries, three miles of wire, gutta percha wire, and insulators.

1 Francis' copper lifeboat.

1 surfboat of copper.

Collection of agricultural implements.

Audubon's Birds, in nine vols.

Natural History of the State of New York, 16 vols.

Annals of Congress, 4 vols.

Laws and Documents of the State of New York.

Journal of the Senate and Assembly of New York.

Lighthouse Reports, 2 vols.

Bancroft's History of the United States, 4 vols.

Farmers' Guide, 2 vols.

1 series of United States Coast Survey Charts.

Morris *Engineering.*

Silver-topped dressing case.

8 yards scarlet broadcloth, and scarlet velvet.

Series of United States standard yard, gallon, bushel, balances and weights.

Quarter cask of Madeira.

Barrel of whiskey.

Box of champagne and cherry cordial and maraschino.

3 boxes of fine tea.

Maps of several states and four large lithographs.

Telescope and stand, in box.

Sheet-iron stove.

An assortment of fine perfumery.

5 Hall rifles.

3 Maynard muskets.

12 cavalry swords.

6 artillery swords.

1 carbine.

20 Army pistols in a box.

Catalogue of New York State Library and of Postoffices.

2 mail bags with padlocks.

FOR THE EMPRESS

Flowered silk embroidered dress.

Toilet dressing-box gilded.

6 dozen assorted perfumery.

---

1. Derived from *Powhatan* log and S. Wells Williams "A Journal of the Perry Expedition to Japan," Asiatic Society of Japan *Transactions,* XXXVII (1910), pages 131–34.

For Commissioner Hayashi

Audubon's *Quadrupeds.*
4 yards scarlet broadcloth.
Clock.
Stove.
Rifle.

Set of Chinaware.
Teaset.
Revolver and powder.
2 dozen assorted perfumery.
20 gallons of whiskey.

1 sword.
3 boxes fine tea.
1 box of champagne.
1 box of finer tea.

For Abe, prince of Ise, first councillor

1 copper lifeboat.
Kendall *War in Mexico* and
    Ripley *History of the
    War in Mexico.*
1 box of champagne.
3 boxes fine tea.

20 gallons whiskey.
1 clock.
1 stove.
1 rifle.

1 sword.
1 revolver and powder.
2 dozen assorted perfumery.
4 yards scarlet broadcloth.

For each of the other five councillors

1 book.[2]
10 gallons of whiskey.
1 lithograph.

1 clock.
1 revolver.
1 rifle.

1 sword.
12 assorted perfumery.

For Ido, prince of Tsushima, second commissioner

Appleton's *Dictionary*
9 assorted perfumery.
Lithograph of New Orleans.
5 gallons whiskey.

1 box of tea.
1 clock.
1 revolver.

1 rifle.
1 sword.
1 box of cherry cordial.

For Izawa, prince of Mimasaki, third commissioner

Model of lifeboat.
View of steamer *Atlantic.*
5 gallons whiskey.
1 rifle.

1 revolver.
1 clock.
1 sword.
9 assorted perfumery.

Box of cherry cordial.
Small box of tea.
Brass howitzer and
    carriages.

For Udono, fourth commissioner

List of post-offices.
Box of tea.
Lithograph of elephant.

9 assorted perfumery.
1 rifle.
1 revolver.
1 clock.

5 gallons whiskey.
1 sword.
Box of cherry cordial.

For Michitaro Matsuzaki, fifth commissioner

Lithograph of a steamer.
1 revolver.
6 assorted perfumery.

1 clock.
1 sword.
5 gallons whiskey.

Box of tea.
Box of cherry cordial.

In addition there was a quantity of tools, agricultural equipment, and seeds for general distribution.

[2] The books thus distributed were Lossing *Field Book of Revolution,* Owen *Architecture, Documentary History of New York,* Downing *Country Houses,* and Owen *Geology of Minnesota.*

APPENDIX D

Some of the Japanese Presents for the Americans

1ST. FOR THE GOVERNMENT OF THE UNITED STATES OF AMERICA, FROM THE EMPEROR

1 gold lacquered writing apparatus.
1 gold lacquered paper box.
1 gold lacquered book case.
1 lacquered writing table.
1 censer of bronze, (cow-shape,) supporting silver flower and stand.
1 set waiters.
1 flower holder and stand.
2 brasiers.
10 pieces fine red pongee.
10 pieces white pongee.
5 pieces flowered crape.
5 pieces red dyed figured crape.

2ND. FROM HAYASHI, 1ST COMMISSIONER

1 lacquered writing apparatus.
1 lacquered paper box.
1 box of paper.
1 box flowered note paper.
5 boxes stamped note and letter paper.
4 boxes assorted sea-shells, 100 in each.
1 box of branch coral and feather in silver.
1 lacquered chow-chow box.
1 box, set of three, lacquered goblets.

7 boxes cups and spoons and goblet cut from conch shells.

3RD. FROM IDO, 2ND COMMISSIONER

2 boxes lacquered waiters, 4 in all.
2 boxes, containing 20 umbrellas.
1 box 30 coir brooms.

4TH. FROM IZAWA, 3RD COMMISSIONER

1 piece red pongee.
1 piece white pongee.
8 boxes, 13 dolls.
1 box bamboo woven articles.
2 boxes bamboo stands.

5TH. FROM UDONO, 4TH COMMISSIONER

3 pieces striped crape.
2 boxes porcelain cups.
1 box, 10 jars of soy.

6TH. FROM MATSUSAKI, 5TH COMMISSIONER

3 boxes porcelain goblets.
1 box figured matting.
35 bundles oak charcoal.

7TH. FROM ABE, 1ST IMPERIAL COUNCILLOR

14 pieces striped-figured silk (taffeta).

8TH–12TH. FROM EACH OF OTHER
5 IMPERIAL COUNCILLORS

10 pieces striped-figured silk (taffeta).

13TH. FROM EMPEROR
TO COMMODORE PERRY

1 lacquered writing apparatus.
1 lacquered paper box.
3 pieces red pongee.
2 pieces white pongee.
2 pieces flowered crape.
3 pieces figured dyed crape.

14TH. FROM COMMISSIONERS
TO CAPT. H. A. ADAMS

3 pieces plain red pongee.
2 pieces dyed figured crape.
20 sets lacquered cups and covers.

15TH–17TH. FROM COMMISSIONERS
TO MR. PERRY, MR. PORTMAN,
AND MR. S. W. WILLIAMS, EACH

2 pieces red pongee.
2 pieces dyed figured crape.
10 sets lacquered cups and covers.

18TH–22ND. FROM COMMISSIONERS
TO MR. GAY, MR. DANBY, MR. DRAPER,
DR. MORROW, AND MR. J. P. WILLIAMS

1 piece red dyed figured crape.
10 sets lacquered cups and covers.

23RD. FROM EMPEROR TO THE
SQUADRON

200 bundles of rice, each 5 Japanese pecks.
300 chickens.

APPENDIX E

Text of the Treaty of Kanagawa

ARTICLE I. There shall be a perfect, permanent, and universal peace, and a sincere and cordial amity, between the United States of America, on the one part, and the Empire of Japan on the other, and between their people, respectively, without exception of persons or places.

ARTICLE II. The port of Shimoda, in the principality of Izu, and the port of Hakodate, in the principality of Matsmai, are granted by the Japanese as ports for the reception of American ships, where they can be supplied with wood, water, provisions, and coal, and other articles their necessities may require, as far as the Japanese have them. The time for opening the first named port is immediately on signing this treaty; the last named port is to be opened immediately after the same day in the ensuing Japanese year.

Note.—A tariff of prices shall be given by the Japanese officers of the things which they can furnish, payment for which shall be made in gold and silver coin.

ARTICLE III. Whenever ships of the United States are thrown or wrecked on the coast of Japan, the Japanese vessels will assist them, and carry their crews to Shimoda or Hakodate, and hand them over to their countrymen appointed to receive them. Whatever articles the shipwrecked men may have preserved shall likewise be restored, and the expenses incurred in the rescue and support of Americans and Japanese who may thus be thrown upon the shores of either nation are not to be refunded.

ARTICLE IV. Those shipwrecked persons and other citizens of the United States shall be free as in other countries, and not subjected to confinement, but shall be amenable to just laws.

ARTICLE V. Shipwrecked men, and other citizens of the United States, temporarily living at Shimoda and Hakodate, shall not be subject to such restrictions and confinement as the Dutch and Chinese are at Nagasaki; but shall be free at Shimoda to go where they please within the limits of seven Japanese miles (or *ri*) from a small island in the harbor of Shimoda, marked on the accompanying chart, hereto appended; and shall in like manner be free to go where they please at Hakodate, within limits to be defined after the visit of the United States squadron to that place.

ARTICLE VI. If there be any other sort of goods wanted, or any business which shall require to be arranged, there shall be careful deliberation between the parties in order to settle such matters.

ARTICLE VII. It is agreed that ships of the United States resorting to the ports open to them shall be permitted to exchange gold and silver coin and articles of goods for other articles of goods, under such regulations as shall be temporarily established by the Japanese government for that purpose. It is stipulated, however, that the ships of the United States shall be permitted to carry away whatever articles they are unwilling to exchange.

ARTICLE VIII. Wood, water, provisions, coal, and goods required, shall only be procured through the agency of Japanese officers appointed for that purpose, and in no other manner.

ARTICLE IX. It is agreed, that if, at any future day, the government of Japan shall grant to any other nation or nations privileges and advantages which are not herein granted to the United States and the citizens thereof, that these same privileges and advantages shall be granted likewise to the United States and to the citizens thereof without any consultation or delay.

ARTICLE X. Ships of the United States shall be permitted to resort to no other ports in Japan but Shimoda and Hakodate, unless in distress or forced by stress of weather.

ARTICLE XI. There shall be appointed by the government of the United States consuls or agents to reside in Shimoda at any time after the expiration of eighteen months from the date of the signing of this treaty; provided that either of the two governments deem such arrangement necessary.

ARTICLE XII. The present convention, having been concluded and duly signed, shall be obligatory, and faithfully observed by the United States of America and Japan, and by the citizens and subjects of each respective power; and it is to be ratified and approved by the President of the United States, by and with the advice and consent of the Senate thereof, and by the august Sovereign of Japan, and the ratification shall be exchanged within eighteen months from the date of the signature thereof, or sooner if practicable.

In faith whereof, we, the respective plenipotentiaries of the United States of America and the Empire of Japan, aforesaid, have signed and sealed these presents.

Done at Kanagawa, this thirty-first day of March, in the year of our Lord Jesus Christ one thousand eight hundred and fifty-four, and of Kayei the seventh year, third month, and third day.

NOTES

Chapter 1: Aliens Arrive

1. Samuel Eliot Morison, *"Old Bruin" Commodore Matthew C. Perry, 1794–1858* (Boston: Little, Brown and Company, 1967), 319.

Chapter 2: The Black Ships of the Evil Men

1. Matthew C. Perry, *Narrative of the Expedition,* Abridged and edited by Sidney Wallach (New York: Coward-McCann, Inc., 1952), 53.
2. See "Letter of the President of the United States to the Emperor of Japan," Appendix A, page 123.
3. In 1846, castaways of the whaler *Lawrence* were imprisoned and cruelly treated for two and a half years until a Dutch ship was permitted to rescue them. When another whaler, the *Lagoda,* was wrecked in 1848, its sixteen survivors were locked in cages so small that they couldn't stand erect. One died and one committed suicide. After being informed of their plight by the Dutch, the United States sent Commander James Glynn to the rescue. In 1849 he sailed an 18-gun ship *Preble* into Nagasaki harbor and refused to budge until the captives were delivered to him. After *Preble,* the next American ships to dock in a Japanese harbor were Commodore Perry's.
4. See Perry, *Narrative of the Expedition,* 148.
5. Ibid., 53.

Chapter 3: His High and Mighty Mysteriousness

1. Perry, *Narrative of the Expedition,* 51. "The Commodore, also, was well aware that the more exclusive he should make himself and the more unyielding he might be in adhering to his declared intentions, the more respect these people of forms and ceremonies would be disposed to award him. Therefore, he deliberately resolved to confer personally with no one but a functionary of the highest rank in the empire."

2. Commodore Perry paid for Oliver's passage to Canton, China. Oliver joined the ship at Hong Kong. The Commodore did this because he did not want to be accused of offering free passage to his son.
3. See Morison, *"Old Bruin,"* 326.
4. See Matthew C. Perry, *The Japan Expedition, 1852–1854, The Personal Journal of Commodore Matthew C. Perry.* Edited by Roger Pineau (Washington, D. C.: Smithsonian Institution Press, 1968), 96.
5. Perry's real title, "Commander-in-Chief, U.S. Naval Forces, East India, China and Japan Seas and Special Ambassador to Japan," should have been sufficient to impress any Oriental potentate!

CHAPTER 4: LANDING ON SACRED SOIL

1. See Perry, *Narrative of the Expedition,* 88.
2. Ibid., 88.
3. Morison, *"Old Bruin,"* 335.

CHAPTER 5: THE DUTCH ISLAND PRISON

1. Von Siebold applied for the job of interpreter on Commodore Perry's expedition but Perry rejected him, suspecting that he was a Russian spy. Perry's hunch may have been correct: Von Siebold joined the Russian expedition, which reached Nagasaki shortly after Perry. Von Siebold subsequently infuriated the Commodore by writing that Russians, not Americans, had opened Japan to the world.

CHAPTER 6: FOREIGNERS FORBIDDEN

1. A number of "Dutch scholars" were reading European books that had been smuggled in through Deshima. They were especially interested in medicine, astronomy, and weaponry. Many scholars expressed their opposition to Japan's isolation policy, not only in the 1850s but also during the first half of the nineteenth century.

CHAPTER 7: THE GREAT PEACE

1. Ruth Benedict, *The Chrysanthemum and the Sword* (New York: New American Library, 1967), 64.
2. Henry Smith, *Learning from Shogun* (Santa Barbara: University of California, 1980), 90.

CHAPTER 8: CLOUDS OVER THE LAND OF THE RISING SUN

1. Ryusaka Tsunoda, et al., *Sources of Japanese Tradition* (New York: Columbia University Press, 1958), 595–597, which contains excerpts of *New Proposals* by Aizawa Seishisai.
2. Richard Storry, *A History of Modern Japan* (Baltimore: Penguin Books, 1960), 89.
3. When Perry came back to Japan in 1854, Yoshida Shoin attempted to stow away, but was apprehended by the Japanese. Yoshida Shoin was imprisoned, released, then imprisoned once more because of his radical ideas. He was beheaded at the age of thirty in 1859.

4. Hirakazu Kaneko, *Manjiro: The Man Who Discovered America* (Boston: Houghton Mifflin Co., 1956), 107–108. Lord Mito also stated, "While there is no justification for doubting the character of Manjiro . . . those barbarians took advantage of his boyhood, bestowed special favors upon him . . . as he had been saved by them [the Americans] and had been under their care from his boyhood until he was twenty years of age, he owes a debt of gratitude to them and, therefore, it is inconceivable that he should act contrary to their interests. Under no circumstances should he be permitted to go on one of the ships to meet those barbarians."

5. Ibid., 88.

6. Ibid., 100.

7. Emily V. Warinner, *Voyager to Destiny* (Indianapolis: The Bobbs-Merrill Co., Inc., 1956), 251–253, and Kaneko, *Manjiro,* 96–98.

8. When Perry returned in 1854, Manjiro translated official documents while being guarded in Edo to prevent him from contacting Americans. After the treaty was signed, Manjiro became an eminent teacher in political and educational circles. He taught navigation and ship engineering and wrote *A Short Cut to English Conversation,* the standard text of the time. He also developed Japan's whaling industry. By the time trade was established with the United States, he helped Westernize Japan. After 1860 Manjiro could be seen wearing his traditional kimono and *hakama* (skirtlike trousers that envelop the kimono up to the waist), an American derby hat, and Western shoes.

CHAPTER 9: THE BLACK SHIPS RETURN

1. Shogun Ieyoshi died on July 27, 1853, just ten days after Perry's first visit ended. He was succeeded by his son, Iesada, who took office on November 22, 1853.

2. See Morison, *"Old Bruin,"* 359.

3. See Warinner, *Voyager to Destiny,* 157.

4. George Henry Preble, *The Opening of Japan: A Diary of Discovery in the Far East, 1853–1856* (Norman, Okla.: University of Oklahoma Press, 1962), 125–126. "The Lieut. Gov. of Uraga told some of our officers of course through interpreters, that when the Treaty was signed we could have plenty of Japanese wives, but said their women did not like mustachios, and hoped when the officers came to see them they would shave them off. From this we have decided that henceforth in Japan, the morality of an officer is to be known by the length of his mustache."

5. Before the Perry expedition left, Patch felt sufficiently safe to visit his family. The Japanese government promised him freedom if he stayed, but he preferred life as an American seaman. Patch subsequently returned to New York State with Jonathan Goble, a shipmate who became a missionary. He and his missionary friend settled in Japan after 1860. Both died there.

CHAPTER 10: THE TREATY HOUSE

1. See Preble, *The Opening of Japan,* 120.

2. Arthur Walworth, *Black Ships Off Japan: The Story of Commodore Perry's Expedition* (Hamden, Conn.: Archon Books, 1966), 172.

CHAPTER 11: AN ARRAY OF GIFTS

1. See Preble, *The Opening of Japan,* 146.
2. Ibid., 146.
3. See Williams, "Journal of the Perry Expedition to Japan," Asiatic Society of Japan, *Transactions* XXXVI (1910): 131–134.
4. See Preble, *The Opening of Japan,* 148–149.
5. See Perry, *Narrative of the Expedition,* 192–194.
6. See Williams, *Transactions,* 131–134.

CHAPTER 12: THE GRAND BANQUET

1. Commodore Perry changed his flagship from the *Susquehanna* to the *Powhatan* after this ship joined his squadron at Hong Kong on August 25, 1853.
2. Decades before Perry arrived some statesmen and political writers were urging the government to consider ending its isolation policy. Because American, British, and Russian ships frequently sailed near their shores, they believed that eventually Japan would have to make a treaty with a foreign power in order to prevent an invasion.
3. See Perry, *The Japanese Expedition,* 188.
4. See Preble, *The Opening of Japan,* page 153.
5. Ibid., 152.
6. Ibid., 152.
7. See Morison, *"Old Bruin,"* 378.

CHAPTER 13: THE TREATY

1. See Morison, *"Old Bruin,"* 380.
2. Edward McCauley, *With Perry in Japan: The Diary of Edward York McCauley* (Princeton, N.J.: 1942), 81.
3. Perry, *Narrative of the Expedition,* 208.

CHAPTER 14: EXCURSIONS ON LAND AND SEA

1. See Preble, *The Opening of Japan,* 123. Preble also wrote, "To inexperienced eyes the dress of the two sexes is so much alike, that but for the manner of wearing their hair, and this custom of staining the teeth, it would be difficult to tell male from female."
2. See Williams, *Transactions,* 131–134.
3. Oliver Statler, *The Black Ship Scroll* (Rutland, Vt.: Charles E. Tuttle Company, 1964), 13.
4. See Perry, *The Japan Expedition,* 200.
5. Ibid., 198.

CHAPTER 15: SHORE LEAVE

1. See Statler, *The Black Ship Scroll,* 15.
2. See Preble, *The Opening of Japan,* 183.

3. See Statler, *The Black Ship Scroll,* 27.

4. See Perry, *Narrative of the Expedition,* 234–235. Commodore Perry ". . . sent an officer on shore in order to quiet the excitement which had been created and to interpose as far as possible in behalf of the poor fellows. . . . If the Commodore had felt himself at liberty to indulge his feelings, he would have gladly given the poor Japanese refuge on board his ship."

5. See Morison, *"Old Bruin,"* 393.

CHAPTER 16: IN THE WAKE OF THE BLACK SHIPS

1. See Howard F. van Zandt, *Pioneer American Merchants in Japan* (Tokyo: Lotus Press Limited, 1980), for a detailed account of the first American civilians in Japan.

AFTERWORD

1. Yonekura Isamu, "The History of the Imperial Family," *The East* (November 1975), 25.

2. Ibid.

ABOUT THE ILLUSTRATIONS

Because of censorship laws, regular newspapers did not exist in Japan in 1853 but handbills, called Kawaraban, were sold in the streets. Each generally consisted of a woodblock illustration and some Japanese reading matter. In addition to anonymous art from these handbills, we have used spot illustrations taken from scrolls that were painted when Comodore Perry visited Japan. Other illustrations reproduce individual works of Japanese art. The design ornament used is the Tokugawa crest.

The American illustrations are reproduced from drawings made, or based on those made, by either William Heine or Eliphalet Brown Jr., unless otherwise noted. Both men were official artists on the Perry expedition.

Illustrations on page 45 courtesy of the Art Institute of Chicago, Nate S. Buckingham Fund; pages 49 and 83 courtesy of the Art Institute of Chicago, Frederick W. Gookin Trust; pages 10, 23, 85, and 91 courtesy of Asahi Shimbun and Kanagawa Prefecture Museum; pages 21, 25, 74, 75, and 79 courtesy of the Chrysler Museum; page 47 courtesy of the Dorothy Segall Collection; page 60 courtesy of the Franklin Delano Roosevelt Library; pages 57, 116, and 117 courtesy of the Heibonsha Press; pages 12, 80, 84, 95, and 96 courtesy of the Historiographical Institute of the University of Tokyo; pages 63, 64, 65, 66, 67, 68, 98, 100, 103, 105(bottom), and 106 courtesy of the Honolulu Academy of Arts, gift of Mrs. Walter F. Dillingham in memory of Alice Perry Grew, 1960; page 38 courtesy of the Kobe City Museum of Namban Art; pages title, 19, 24, 27, 32–33, 55, 70–71, 72, 73, 81(bottom), 88–89, 101, 102, 105(top), 109, and 118 reproduced from the collections of the Library of Congress; pages 15 and 56 courtesy of the Metropolitan Museum of Art, Bashford Dean Memorial Collection; pages 17, 35, and 81(top) courtesy of the National Archives; pages 108 and 111 courtesy of the New York Public Library, Astor, Lenox, and Tilden Foundations; pages 50 and 115 courtesy of the New York Public Library, Spencer Collection; page 52 courtesy of the Philadelphia Art Museum.

BIBLIOGRAPHY

Barr, Pat. *The Coming of the Barbarians*. New York: E. P. Dutton, Inc., 1967.

Benedict, Ruth. *The Chrysanthemum and the Sword*. New York: New American Library, 1967.

Chamberlain, Basil Hall. *Japanese Things*. Rutland, Vt.: Charles E. Tuttle Company, 1971.

Dilts, Marion May. *The Pageant of Japanese History*. New York: Longmans, Green and Co., 1961.

————. *Two Japans*. New York: David McKay Company, Inc., 1963.

Dunn, C. J. *Everyday Life in Traditional Japan*. Rutland, Vt.: Charles E. Tuttle Company, 1976.

Hall, John Whitney. *Japan from Prehistory to Modern Times*. New York: Delacorte Press, 1970.

————, and Jansen, Marius B., eds. *Studies in the Institutional History of Early Modern Japan*. Princeton, N.J.: Princeton University Press, 1968.

Kaneko, Hirakazu. *Manjiro: The Man Who Discovered America*. Boston: Houghton Mifflin Co., 1956.

Keene, Donald. *The Japanese Discovery of Europe, 1720–1830*. Stanford, Calif.: Stanford University Press, 1969.

Koestler, Arthur: *The Lotus and the Robot*. New York: Harper & Row, 1960.

Lach, Donald F., and Flaumenhaft, Carol, eds. *Asia on the Eve of Europe's Expansion*. Englewood Cliffs, N.J.: Prentice-Hall, Inc., 1965.

McCauley, Edward. *With Perry in Japan: The Diary of Edward York McCauley*. Princeton, N.J.: 1942.

Morison, Samuel Eliot. *"Old Bruin" Commodore Matthew C. Perry, 1794–1858*. Boston: Little, Brown and Company, 1967.

Perrin, Noel. *Giving Up the Gun: Japan's Reversion to the Sword, 1543–1879*. Boston: David R. Godine, 1979.

Perry, Matthew C. *Narrative of the Expedition of an American Squadron to the China Seas and Japan Under the Command of Commodore M.C. Perry, United States Navy, Compiled at His Request and Under His Supervision, By Francis L. Hawks, D.D., L.L.D.* Abridged and edited by Sidney Wallach. New York: Coward-McCann, Inc., 1952.

————. *The Japan Expedition 1852–1854, The Personal Journal of Commodore Matthew C. Perry*. Edited by Roger Pineau. Washington, D.C.: Smithsonian Institution Press, 1968.

Preble, George Henry. *The Opening of Japan: A Diary of Discovery in the Far East, 1853–1856*. Edited by Boleslaw Szczesniak. Norman, Okla.: University of Oklahoma Press, 1962.

Reischauer, Edwin O. *Japan: The Story of a Nation*. Rev. ed. Tokyo: Charles E. Tuttle Company, 1976.

Rudofsky, Bernard. *The Kimono Mind.* Garden City, N.Y.: Doubleday and Company, Inc., 1965.

Sansom, George. *A History of Japan, 1615–1867.* Stanford, Calif.: Stanford University Press, 1963.

————. *The Western World and Japan.* New York: Alfred A. Knopf, 1950.

Smith, Henry. *Learning from Shogun.* Santa Barbara: University of California, 1980.

Statler, Oliver. *The Black Ship Scroll.* Rutland, Vt.: Charles E. Tuttle Company, 1964.

————. *Japanese Inn.* Honolulu: University of Hawaii Press, 1961.

————. *Shimoda Story.* New York: Random House, 1969.

Storry, Richard. *A History of Modern Japan.* Baltimore: Penguin Books, 1960.

Taylor, Bayard. *A Visit to India, China and Japan.* New York: Putnam, 1855.

Tsunoda, Ryusaku; De Bary, W. Theodore; and Keene, Donald. *Sources of Japanese Tradition.* New York: Columbia University Press, 1958.

Van Zandt, Howard F. *Pioneer American Merchants in Japan.* Tokyo: Lotus Press Limited, 1980.

Von Siebold, Dr. Philip Franz. *Manners and Customs of the Japanese.* (1st edition Harper & Bros., New York, 1841.) Rutland, Vt.: Charles E. Tuttle Company, 1981.

Walworth, Arthur. *Black Ships Off Japan: The Story of Commodore Perry's Expedition.* Hamden, Conn.: Archon Books, 1966.

Warinner, Emily V. *Voyager to Destiny.* Indianapolis: The Bobbs-Merrill Co., Inc., 1956.

Webb, Herschel. *The Japanese Imperial Institution in the Tokugawa Period.* New York: Columbia University Press, 1968.

Williams, S. Wells. "Journal of the Perry Expedition to Japan." Asiatic Society of Japan: *Transactions* XXXVII (1910): 131–134.

Yonekura, Isamu. "The History of the Imperial Family," *The East* (November 1975).

INDEX

Italicized numerals indicate illustrations.